Gardening

WITH THE EXPERTS

HERBS

Gardening WITH THE EXPERTS

HERBS

ROSA VALLANCE

Bloomsbury Books
London

Photographs: Mary Moody: front cover, pages 6, 11, 14.
Manuel Patty: pages 7, 9, 13, 15, 16 (above and below right), 19, 21 (above), 26,27, (below left), 31, 34, 36.
Weldon Trannies: opposite title page, pages 8, 12, 16 (below left), 17, 18, 20, 21 (below),
22, 23, 24-25, 27,(above and below right), 28, 29, 30, 32.

Published by Harlaxton Publishing Ltd
2 Avenue Road, Grantham, Lincolnshire, NG31 6TA, United Kingdom.
A Member of the Weldon International Group of Companies.

First published in 1990 (Limp)
Reprint 1991 (Cased)
Reprint 1992 (Cased)

© Copyright Harlaxton Publishing Ltd
© Copyright design Harlaxton Publishing Ltd

This edition published in 1993 by
Bloomsbury Books
an imprint of
The Godfrey Cave Group
42 Bloomsbury Street, London. WC1B 3QJ
under license from Harlaxton Publishing Ltd.

Publishing Manager: Robin Burgess
Illustrations: Kathie Baxter Smith
Typeset in UK by Seller's, Grantham
Produced in Singapore by Imago

British Library Cataloguing-in-Publication data.
A catalogue record for this book is available from the British Library.
Title: Gardening with the Experts: Herbs.
ISBN:1 85471 186 5

CONTENTS

INTRODUCTION

The word 'herb' refers to any of that host of plants, both herbaceous and woody, whose leaves, flowers, seeds, roots, bark and other parts we use for decoration, flavour, fragrance, medicine, cosmetics and dyes.

Most herbaceous plants have soft and succulent rather than woody stems, they include many vegetables along with flowers, shrubs, trees, weeds and grasses. The name 'herb' derives from the Latin *herba* which means grass or green crops.

Their practicality and attractiveness make herbs a valuable asset in any garden. Tradition has dictated that herbs be planted as a separate group, either in an informal or formal herb garden or without much imagination alongside edibles in the vegetable garden. But times are changing!

We are now experiencing a 'herban renewal'— a renaissance of interest in herbs because of our awareness of natural and healthy foods and creative cooking, as well as a resurgence of nostalgia.

Most people, after discovering the pleasure and economy of home-grown produce, start out with a few basic herbs and are soon eager to try others. Nurseries are responding to this interest with a larger selection of new varieties and with more of the old species.

Today, herbs are putting in appearances as part of the total garden landscape. They are happily visible alongside bulbs, annuals, perennials and shrubs. Other ways that herbs can be incorporated into the overall garden picture are as borders or edging around flower beds; among annuals and perennials in blooming borders; as fillers for corners and empty pockets between

A herb garden.

6

Lavender in a garden bed.

other plants; and as ground covers or fragrant carpeting.

Herbs combine well with plants that are usually grown in rock gardens, they thrive on hillsides and slopes or cascading over terraces. You can use them to subdue brilliant colours, selecting grey or silver-foliage species and tucking them alongside other plants so long as their cultivation is compatible.

Then there are container-grown herbs to move about at will, baskets or hanging pots to suspend from roof overhangs, tree branches, fences or walls.

Herbs can be grown in very small spaces. Plant creeping herbs between paving stones; remove a few bricks from a walkway and soften the area with creeping, fragrant herbs; or half-bury hollow cement blocks, then fill them with plants to add interest to an open area.

There is no need to think of herbs as weedy garden plants or a few straggly plants in pots on the kitchen window-sill.

HOW TO GROW HERBS: THE BASICS

The three requirements for successfully growing herbs as well as many other plants are: light, food and good drainage.

In spite of all the lore surrounding the use of herbs, growing them is no more difficult than growing ordinary flowers or vegetables. Think of them as part of the vegetable garden. Most plants classed as herbs are hardy, easy to grow, practically immune to diseases and pests, adaptable to many types of soil and growing conditions, and quite tolerant of drought and neglect.

Like any group of plants, your attention to their simple wants and needs will be amply rewarded. Most herbs need sunlight for at least five hours a day. Some are tolerant to partial shade and some woodland natives enjoy full shade. Check the requirements of individual plants in the section on "Where to Plant Herbs".

Page opposite: Herbs in a decorative pot.   *Above: **Sorrel** prefers well-mulched soil.*

IMPROVING DRAINAGE

In heavy soils, mix coarse grit or sand into the top 45 centimetres. Add compost for fibre to increase bacterial activity. This will make more plant nutrients available. It will also attract earthworm activity which will lighten and further enrich the soil.

Most herbs, like vegetables, prefer a slightly alkaline soil. A light sprinkling of lime or wood ash will help to tone down an acidic soil. Avoid using artificial fertilisers as these can make growth too lush, that eventually results in poor flavour and often reduce the amounts of fragrant oils stored in the leaves.

If your soil is poor you might like to try the some of the suggestions in the "Herbal Fertilisers" section.

Should your soil be very waterlogged or prone to becoming waterlogged, a raised bed might be a permanent solution. These are traditional in herb gardening and also defines areas, allow access for weeding or harvesting and permit access for the infirm in wheelchairs.

PREPARING THE SOIL

Many herbs will survive on poor, stony ground, but they generally prefer a light, slightly sandy soil with good drainage.

In a new bed, prepare the soil in early spring before sowing or planting. Dig deeply, then over several weeks remove persistent weeds and those with taproots. Create a fine tilth, then rake it to a level surface. Let the soil settle for atleast a week before planting seed. However, pot-grown herbs can be planted immediately.

MULCHING

Once herbs are established, mulching will help to prevent soil drying out too quickly and will provide nutrients, especially helpful during the plants' growing season.

A covering of organic matter such as pea straw, rotted hay or bark chip, spread over the soil and around plants, will control weed growth, keep the soil at a cooler and more even temperature as well as visually enhance the plant setting.

Plastic sheeting will tend to make the soil's surface retain too much moisture, it does not allow air circulation, so the soil quickly sours.

If the soil is very moist, those herbs that prefer drier positions, such as mallows or evening primrose, might be happier with a surround of gravel rather than mulch.

PROPAGATION AND PLANTING

You should now be holding and supporting the plant and roots. Slip the plant into the hole, making sure that the soil will come to the same level on the stem as it was in the container, that the soil level is the same as the surrounding soil. Add a little more soil and firm it down gently to eliminate air

Seed and plantlets of common herbs are available at garden centres, nurseries and plant shops, herb societies, herb-growing friends and mail order catalogues .

An enormous number of herbs, both common and rare, can be grown from seed, but if you require only one or two plants it is often more economical and certainly quicker to buy them. When you wish to pop your store-bought or given treasure into the garden, water the soil well beforehand or let the herb soak in a bucket of water for half an hour or so to ensure that the soil and root system hold together.

Make a hole in the soil large enough for the plant's roots. Now turn the pot upside down, with a finger on each side of the stem and touching the soil, give the edge of the pot a sharp rap on the side of a bench.

Parsley *seeds should be sown in situ.*

11

pockets. Water the firmed soil to help your new plant settle in. If you know the name of the herb, insert a label into the soil.

For a head start on the growing season or if it is rare or expensive seed, seedlings may be grown indoors. This way, all conditions can be controlled. It is not advisable to start plants with long taproots, such as parsley, indoors unless they are grown in separate large containers, and even then they do not transplant easily.

Use a proprietary loamless, seed-growing mix or mix your own using:

2 parts sterilised and sieved loam
1 part peat or leaf mould
1 part coarse sand
20 grams lime

Blend well and pass through an 8mm sieve. A shallow seed tray (5cm deep) or any flat, clean container that has good drainage may be used for small seed. With small sowings use small pots for economy of soil and space. If using deeper containers, first fill with clean drainage material such as gravel or broken crock. Add growing mix to within 10mm of the top.

Give the tray or pot a sharp downward tap. Then press the soil surface gently with a flat board. If the mix is very dry, water and leave it to drain.

Sow seed thinly, mixing fine seed with a bit of sand for even distribution. Sprinkle a fine layer of potting mix over the seed.

Larger seeds should be covered with a layer as deep as the seed width. In both cases, press the soil down gently and level it if necessary. Carefully and lightly mist the soil with water and date the planting. Cover the container with glass or plastic, or enclose it in a large plastic bag.

It should not be necessary to water again until sprouting begins, but open the cover

A variety of herbs can be grown together in a container.

every day for about an hour to let in fresh air and prevent moisture build-up. If dry spots appear on the soil before sprouting commences, set the containers in water (rather than watering them from above which will probably flush the seedlings out of the soil) until the soil is damp.

When sprouting begins, take the cover off and place the container in indirect light for several days. When the first pair of true leaves has formed, after the cotyledons (the two seed leaves which initially emerge), thin the plantlets out or transplant them to a larger pot to prevent overcrowding.

Fill the new container with prepared seedling mix. Handle the transplants by their leaves to prevent bruising or breaking the tiny roots and stems. Using a 'dibbler' or pencil, make a small hole in the soil of the new container and set in the seedling so its leaves are 5cm above the surface. Firm down the soil and water lightly. Set the pot in indirect sunlight.

When the seedlings have grown, remove any weaker subjects, leaving the strongest to continue growing. This will secure the best of the species. The herbs can now be planted in larger pots or out in the garden if there is no danger of frosts.

To avoid shock when planting out, try to pick a calm, warm day, avoiding hot, windy or rainy days. Cloches or light shelter are recommended for the early growing stages outdoors in order to protect the plants from winds, unexpected frost and birds.

SOWING OUTDOORS

Annuals are best sown where you wish them to grow, as root disturbance through transplanting can make them bolt to seed.

Germination depends on three requirements: water, air and warmth. Generally, seed is sown mid to late spring after the soil

Foeniculum vulgare (fennel)

has warmed, or in early autumn.

For spring sowing, new weed seedlings appearing in the garden are a good indication that the time is right for your sowing. Remove the weeds and sow the seed thinly either in shallow drills or freshly prepared beds. Scatter the seed evenly (if very fine, mix it with sand for better distribution) over the area.

Cover the seed thinly with soil and tap it down gently. Water with a fine spray. Label your beds as soon as you have planted them so you will know what is growing where. (Dill and fennel look very similar early on.) Keep the soil moist but never soggy.

Normally annuals take two weeks and perennials about three to four weeks to germinate. Parsley is notoriously slow, taking at least six weeks for germination, so be patient.

For a continuous harvest of short-cycle

herbs such as coriander and borage, make successive sowings several weeks apart. You will sometimes find that seed sown at the same time comes up in batches at various spots. This is a natural protective mechanism for survival of the species and is particularly noticeable in some wild herbs. These herbs will grow only at certain times of the year.

PROPAGATION FROM CUTTINGS, DIVISION AND LAYERING

Cuttings are the most certain way to get plants similar in flower colour and leaf shape to the parent plant. The parent plant gets a beneficial trim in the process. This method is often faster than germination from seed. It is also the most inexpensive and rewarding way to expand your herb collection. Keen herb growers are generally happy to give or exchange cuttings with other growers.

You will need a source of plants, secateurs or a sharp knife, a clear plastic bag, damp paper towelling or something similar to keep cut ends moist (prevent wilting), coarse sand, pumice, peat or propagation mix, pots or deep seed trays.

The three types of cuttings follow the same method of propagation.

Softwood or tip cuttings are taken from non-woody plants. Choose strong new shoots without flower buds.

When taking tip cuttings, cut straight across a shoot so that it is 5 to 10cm in length, with four or five leaf joints. Trim the stem back to just beneath a leaf joint.

Softwood cuttings can be taken most of the year, especially in late spring or after flowering, but not in winter.

Try artemisias or balm, basil, mint, sage, thyme or hyssop.

Semi-hardwood and hardwood cuttings are taken from woody shrubs and trees.

Curry plant, rosemary, rue, santolina, French tarragon and winter savory fall into this category.

With semi-hardwood cuttings, cut pieces 10 to 15cm in length, with hardwoods, 15 to 40cm long. Trim these just below the lowest leaf bud. Hardwood cuttings can be taken from herbs such as lemon verbena from mid to late autumn.

Heel cuttings are taken from shrubby herbs such as rosemary, sage and lavender.

Use a new branch that is starting to firm at the base where it joins the main stem. Pull the branch with a downward movement so that the heel of the older wood of

Mint

the main stem is attached. Using secateurs or a sharp knife, trim the heel, leaving a neat sliver of older wood across the base.

Take heel cuttings from mid-summer to mid-autumn.

For all methods, strip the leaves from the lower third of the cutting before planting, take care not to tear the stem.

If planting outside, choose a warm and sheltered spot, if possible out of direct sunlight. Firmly plant the cutting with the cut side down in gritty or peaty soil, keep it moist. An ideal spot might be under the mother plant.

With container planting, place a third of the length of the cuttings in the potting medium, either singly or with several around the edge of the pot, water, then

PROPAGATION FROM CUTTINGS

1.TAKE CUTTINGS WITH SHARP SECATEURS. 2.INSERT CUTTINGS INTO CLEAN POTS. 3.WATER THOROUGHLY. 4.ENCLOSE POTS IN CLEAR PLASTIC UNTIL ROOTED.

Basil

cover them with a plastic bag raised above the leaves to prevent mildew.

This will provide the cuttings with the moisture and warmth that will speed up the rooting process. Open the bag every few days to allow fresh air to enter and to prevent mould build-up.

When the foliage seems to perk up, the bag may be removed. As soon as signs of new growth are noticed (this may be one month for tender-stemmed herbs such as sage, to several months for woody stemmed varieties), transfer the plants to containers and place these in a sheltered spot with indirect sunlight, gradually increasing exposure to direct sunlight over a period of two weeks. Apply weak liquid fertiliser or compost for plant nutrients.

Hardwood cuttings will develop over the winter and ought to be ready for spring planting. If a plant's roots show at the base of the container, transplant it to a larger pot or plant it in a permanent position.

Root Cutting propagation of Lemon balm, sage, rosemary and comfrey can be carried out in spring and autumn.

Sage

Dig up the plant and remove pieces of root 5cm in diameter that have bud growth. Cut these pieces into 5cm long sections and discard the thin ends.

Place these vertically into moistened potting mix in a container and cover with 5cm of sand. Cover with a plastic bag and follow the procedure for tip cuttings until there are signs of growth.

When the plants have gained substantial growth, they can be repotted or planted out in the garden,

Root Division is a simple method of severing the roots so that some top growth remains attached to each piece.

This is usually done with plants that grow in clumps, such as costmary, yarrow, mint, lemon balm, lady's bedstraw and

Rosemary

Bergamot

bergamot. Division checks the spread of these herbs and keeps them hardier, besides giving the keen gardener multiple plants for replanting or giving away.

Division is best attempted either in spring, before there is much new growth, or in autumn, after plants become dormant.

Simply wet the soil around the plant, dig it up or take it out of its pot, separate the plant into sections by pulling it apart with your fingers or with two forks back to back, or by cutting through sections with a spade or secateurs.

Make sure each section has a growing point and some roots. Discard hard old growth and tidy up the plant as you go.

Replant the sections in the ground or in containers. Keep the soil moist until the plants adjust to their new situations.

Layering is pegging down or covering with soil, part of a stem from the mother plant. Many plants, such as thyme will often do this naturally.

Bend a stem that will touch the earth just below a leaf node about 10cm from the growing tip. Peg it to the ground with bent wire or a short, forked branch so that contact is made with the soil. Keep this area moist. Check for root development in six weeks.

When roots are established, cut the stem from the parent just above the new roots. Dig up the roots and stem then plant them in a container or directly in the garden.

If you attempt this in autumn and your region experiences frosts, cover the contact point with mulch to prevent damage from unexpected frosts.

A clump of pennyroyal seedlings being separated by root division.

Thyme

Mound Layering of plants such as sage and thyme, which can become woody in the centre, can be improved in appearance or propagated in spring by mounding soil over the woody centre until only young growth shows.

Check in eight weeks for new roots at the base of the shoots. When the roots are established, cut the rooted shoot from the parent plant and proceed as for layering.

Lemon balm

WHERE TO PLANT HERBS

HERBS FOR DRY GROUND

Dry ground, walls and earthen banks are ideal environments for most culinary and aromatic herbs as many originate fromthe Mediterranean, often in harsh scrub land.

The volatile oils and flavours are a product of the sun and set by warm winds. These herbs have developed colours and tough leaves to conserve moisture which otherwise, the winds would draw out and the sun would evaporate. To repel browsing animals, the plants have developed spiky tips, leathery surfaces and volatile oils which form a protective vapour around the plant. These characteristics together with their pungent flavours ensure some survival from herbivores.

To imitate their natural environment, a stony, well-drained garden bed, a sunny position and a not-too-rich soil is ideal.

Tropaeolum majus (Nasturtiums) thrive in rockeries or in the crevices of walls.

Lavender growing on top of a wall.

For walls or rockeries, any herb with 'wall' in its name is an obvious choice, such as wall germander or wallflower.

Others you might like to try in crevices or on top of a sunny wall are nasturtiums, perennial chamomile, and any prostrate form of catmint, rosemary, sage or savory. For the very top of a wall, hyssop, santolina and lavender are very suitable.

For really dry corners where the soil is poor and thin, only the most tolerant and toughest of herbs, bugloss*, mugwort, species of mallow, mullein, yarrow, evening primrose or white horehound will survive.

Other herbs suitable for dry environ-ments are artemisias, curry plant, costmary, fennel, lady's bedstraw, hypericum*, musk mallow, marjorams, weld, rue, meadow clary, salad burnet, betony, feverfew, tansy and vervain.

HERBS FOR SHADY PLACES

Many woodland herbs will grow well in the shade of a wall or beneath a tree.

Generally, these will be perennials that flower early and continue to have interest-ing foliage, a bonus when spring flowering is over. This is an important consideration for your overall garden plan.

For heavy shade: bugle, woodruff, pennyroyal, evening primrose, lungwort valerian and sweet violet.

For partial shade: lady's mantle, angelica, foxglove, wild strawberry, ground ivy, sweet cicely, wood sage and orris.

For light shade: chives, marshmallow, chervil, foxglove, rocket, meadowsweet, lady's bedstraw, hypericum, musk mallow, lemon balm, the mints, the parsleys and comfrey.

* These herbs are considered noxious weeds in some regions. Please check with your local authority before planting them.

Sweet marjoram (above) and salad burnet (below).

HERBS FOR WATERY SURROUNDS AND DAMP GROUND

Very few herbs need a really muddy place in the garden. A reasonably water retentive soil is usually sufficient.

These herbs will tolerate light or dappled shade. Most have medicinal or household uses and they are generally perennials. Unlike woodland plants, they will begin to blossom from early summer onwards.

Comfrey and elecampane will survive in a patch of heavy, damp soil if nothing else seems to grow. These are the most tolerant of herbs, growing in spreading clumps to large-sized plants. For fragrant flowers in early summer, valerian, agrimony and meadowsweet do admirably. Sweet cicely, with its soft green, fernlike leaves, will put on a delicate show of white flowers in early spring in a damp spot or beneath a tree.

Other herbs for damp spots are angelica, sneezewort, marshmallow and soapwort .

Above: A lightly shaded area is suitable for peppermint.
*Page opposite: Foxgloves (**digitalis**) prefer partial or light shade.*

HERBS FOR VARIOUS PURPOSES

SCENT

Scented flowers: These include evening primrose, lady's bedstraw, lavenders, lemon verbena, meadowsweet, mignonette, sages, rocket, chives, bergamot, calendula, chamomile, mallow and valerian, some with delicate scents and some with powerful smells.

Scents are very personal preferences, and what one individual finds pleasant another may find abhorrent.

Check with your nose when buying herbs.

Scented foliage: These herbs are lovely when planted where they will be brushed against. They will release their fragrance when they are touched or picked:

Agrimony, angelica, artemisias, anise, anise hyssop, balm of Gilead, basils, sweet bay, bergamot, camphor, caraway, catmint, chamomile, chervil, coriander, costmary, dill, fennel, lavenders, lemon balm, lemon grass, lemon verbena, lovage, marjorams, oregano, pyrethrum, rosemary, rue, sages,

Evening primrose produces scented flowers.

26

Crossroads Books
1935 Main Street
Watsonville CA 95076
403-728-4139
Transaction No: 67357
09/29/97 15:49:01   CLERK:

```
1 @  3.99 1854711865                    3.99
   Gardening with Herbs
SUBTOTAL                                3.99
TAX @ 8.000%                            0.32
TOTAL                                   4.31
CHECK                                   4.31
Total Tendered        $                 4.31
CHECK Credit                            0.00
```

THANK YOU!
Save Money Everyday

Join the Crossroads Book Club

Anise has fragrant foliage

santolina, savories, sweet cicely, tansy, thymes, tarragon, curry and motherwort, to name but some.

To entice bees: These herbs planted in full sun will ensure a long flowering period and a steady stream of busy, workers—anise hyssop, balm of Gilead, bergamot, betony, borage, caraway, catmint, catnip, hyssop, lavenders, lemon balm, lungwort, marjoram, mignonette, rosemary, sages, savories and thymes.

To repel insects: The following do an

Oregano leaves are strongly scented.

Bees are attracted to the caraway plant.

admirable job in the garden and home—artemisias, basils, chives, feverfew, garlic, mint, pyrethrum, rue, santolina, tansy.

EDGES, HEDGES, LAWNS AND GROUND COVERS

For edges: Alpine strawberry, basils, chives, wall germander, dwarf lavenders, marjorams, parsleys, dwarf rosemary, rue, sages, salad burnet, savories, thyme, violets.

For hedges: Sweet bay, common sage, curry plant, hyssop, lavenders, rosemary.

For lawns: Lawn chamomile, pennyroyal and the smaller thymes.

For ground covers: Bugle, chamomile, ground ivy, lady's bedstraw, Corsican mint, nasturtiums, oregano, pennyroyal, prostrate rosemary, prostrate winter savory, sweet woodruff and wild thymes.

FOLIAGE COLOUR

Silver or grey leaves: Use these to lighten a dark corner, to contrast with darker colours or to break up a colour scheme. They are very effective in mass plantings. The artemisias, camphor, catmint, clary sage, costmary, curry plant, white horehound, lavenders, mullein, pyrethrum, rue, common sage, santolina, and orange and woolly thyme.

Darker leaves: With red leaves — purple basil, bronze fennel, red sage; with green leaves — anthemis (dyer's chamomile), wall germander, ground ivy, meadowsweet, rosemary, some thymes.

Yellow or orange leaves: Aureum marjoram, aureum feverfew and some varieties of thyme.

The colour of Yarrow flowers varies with the species.

FLOWER COLOUR

White or cream: Anise, applemint, basil, borage, caraway, curry plant, lemon balm, garlic chives, Roman chamomile, meadowsweet, woodruff, orris, musk mallow, sweet marjoram, sweet cicely, Welsh comfrey, feverfew, winter savory and some yarrows.

Yellow or orange: Agrimony, calendula, dyer's chamomile, chamomile, lady's bedstraw, curry plant, feverfew, hypericum, elecampane, evening primrose, santolina, nasturtiums, tansy, mullein, woad, yarrow.

Blue or mauve: Anise hyssop, betony, borage, bugle, catmint, chives, hyssop, most lavenders, lungwort, some mints, orris, rosemary, sage, some thymes, violets.

Pink or red: Balm of Gilead, some basils, bergamot, betony, comfrey, coriander, lungwort, marshmallow, musk mallow, golden marjoram, motherwort, pineapple sage, red sage, summer savory, soapwort, some thymes, valerian and red yarrow.

Green-yellow: Lady's mantle, dill, fennel, lady's bedstraw, lovage, weld, rue.

HEIGHT

As the height of plants can determine the focal point of a garden, the eye is led to distances, to mark corners, note steps or seats, or windbreaks where they are needed or provided.

The following list gives plants in order of height (with the tallest first):

Evergreen trees and shrubs: Sweet bay 7m, box 3m, rosemary 2.5m, lavender 1.2m

The evergreen shrub southernwood is often grown in cottage gardens.

apothecary rose 1.2m, Jerusalem sage 1.2m, wormwood 1m, southernwood 90cm, santolina 80cm, sage 75cm, curry plant 60cm.

Perennial herbs: Elecampane 2m, lovage 2m, sweet cicely 1.5m, valerian 1.5m, comfrey 1.5m, mugwort 1.5m, tansy 1.5m, catnip 1.5m, meadowsweet 1m, fennel 1m, marshmallow 1m, vervain 1m.

Biennial herbs: Angelica 2m, mullein 2m, weld 1.5m, clary sage 1.2m, evening primrose 1m.

Annual herb: Dill 1.5m.

CONTAINER HERBS

There are times when, through preference, for ease of access, for confinement, for a plant's survival or because of lack of garden space, container planting really comes into its own. You can prolong the growing season of herbs, place them where they can appeal to your sense of smell, and create a visually appealing environment which is a constant source of interest.

Pots of herbs look attractive when grouped.

Although herbs thrive more vigorously in the ground, with a certain amount of care and commonsense you can grow them in pots, either indoors or outdoors.

When placing containers on balconies or freestanding structures, take care that these can support the weighty combination of soil and water. Exposure to the wind must also be considered. Small containers may be blown over and tender-leaved herbs can be quickly damaged by strong winds.

Herbs in a group of pots can provide a focal point and look more pleasing to the eye than one lonely specimen. They seem to enjoy each other's company and benefit from the microclimate that grouping creates. By changing the position of the pots, you can fill seasonal gaps or vary the appearance of your garden. Herbs in pots are an excellent way to create different colour schemes in small or large areas. A silver or moonlight garden would have artemisias, santolinas and curry plants; a golden garden would have lemon thyme, variegated sage, variegated lemon balm, calendula, lady's bedstraw and nasturtiums; a blue garden would have hyssop, borage, catmint, rosemary and sage.

The space needed by particular plants will dictate how many can be put in a planter. A metre-long container can hold four or five low-growing herbs, such as sage, thyme, marjoram and salad burnet,

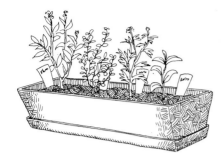

which will benefit from being kept well trimmed. A delightful addition to a barbecue area is a tub or barrel filled with culinary herbs such as rosemary, chives, sage, mint (in its own container) or lemon balm, to add colour and fragrance to outdoor entertaining.

Remember, these plants are dependent

A wall planter with violets

on your care and more vulnerable than plants in the open ground. Some general rules for successful container planting are as follows:

1. Always start with a clean pot. Wash the pot with hot water and washing soda or soap, or with a weak solution of household bleach, rinsing well.
2. Provide the plants with good drainage. For seedlings, add some coarse pumice to the bottom of the pot.
3. Make sure that the soil is friable and porous. Do not use ordinary garden soil. A good commercial potting mix is suitable for older plants but is often too rich for tiny seedlings. Traditional potting compound can be made by combining 7 parts loam, 3 parts peat and 2 parts gritty or sharp sand with some well-rotted compost. Do not use builder's sand since it will become compact, making drainage worse. Keep the mixture loose and open to prevent fungal spore formation.
4. Ensure that the sizes of the container and the plant are compatible. Small plants flounder in large pots.
5. Check regularly for aphids and thrips and deal with these pests if infestation is present. See the "Herbal Insecticides" section in this book.
6. Monitor indoor herbs regularly for their need for watering. Do not water them unnecessarily but never allow them to become bone dry. Rosemary never fully recovers if it dries out totally, yet sage will collapse if watered too frequently. Overwatering can cause rootrot by eliminating vital air pockets, needed by root hairs. An occasional spray with tepid water from a mister is useful in hot weather for soft-leaved herbs such as basil.

7. Remove deadheads, trim the leaves back and keep the pot weed-free to aid vigorous growth.

8. Feed herbs through their leaves or the soil every two weeks during the growing season, easing off as the growth rate slows and stop altogether during the dormant period.

9. Meet the herbs' light requirements but do not let the pots get too hot.

10. If a herb looks sad, check if it needs water, less water or food, whether it is sitting in a draught or whether it is receiving the correct amount of light.

Mint should be grown in its own container.

HERBAL FERTILISERS

Comfrey: One comfrey plant will provide four crops a year. Comfrey fertiliser supplies nitrogen, phosphorus, potash and trace elements. Method: Pick the leaves from late spring to midsummer. Let them wilt for at least forty-eight hours, mulch them and apply the mulch directly to plants, or soak fresh leaves in water for four weeks and use the liquid as a fertiliser.

Dill: This is rich in potassium, sulphur, sodium and other minerals.

Tansy: Tansy is rich in potassium and other minerals.

Yarrow: This provides copper and is a good general fertiliser.

Basic Recipe: Pour 1 litre of boiling

water over a handful of fresh herbs or over 30 grams of dried herbs, cover, infuse for ten minutes and strain before using.

Do not use aluminium vessels.

HERBAL INSECTICIDES

Basil leaves can be used to repel aphids. For method, see chamomile flowers below.

Costmary leaves can be used as a general insecticide. For method, see chamomile flowers below.

Wormwood leaves should be used only on mature plants (because of its toxicity) against larger pests such as caterpillars, moths, flea beetles and aphids.
Method: Put 15 grams of dried herbs in 1 litre of cold water. Simmer covered for half an hour. Turn heat off and steep for fifteen minutes. Do not use aluminium vessels.

Chamomile flowers prevent damping off in seedlings. Method: Pour 1 litre of boiling water over 30 ml of dried flowers or over a handful of fresh flowers. Cover, steep for ten minutes, strain and use at once.

Pyrethrum is a natural insecticide which rapidly paralyses insects. Its flower heads can be dried or powdered and used against all common sucking insects: bedbugs, mosquitoes, cockroaches and domestic fly. Prolonged contact with the flower heads can cause allergic reactions in some people, so rubber gloves are a must. Method: Pick the open flower heads. Dry and pulverise them. To make a spray, steep 30 grams of powder in 50 ml of methylated spirits. Dilute this with 18 litres of water.

Proprietary brands of this insecticide are also available. Spray the insecticide at dusk so that plants and bees will be safe. The solution will have dispersed by morning, especially if exposed to bright sunlight.

Chamomile flowers help to prevent damping-off in seedlings.

THE HARVEST

PICKING AND HARVESTING

After spending time sowing and planting, herb gardeners reap their just rewards.

Most culinary herbs can be used from the seedling stage, as their flavours are already present. Keep in mind that, as you snip and pick, you are determining the future shape of the growing plant. If you harvest leaves judiciously, the plant will become fuller and bushier.

Evergreen herbs, such as sage, thyme, basil, tarragon and marjoram, maintain a bushier shape if the growing tip is pinched out first. In general, do not remove more than a fifth of the herb's leaves in order to allow regeneration and growth of the plant.

When harvesting for preserving ensure that the herbs have not been sprayed recently with pesticides or herbicides. (If they have been sprayed, wait the time recommended by the manufacturer's instructions before harvesting.)

For maximum flavour preservation, harvest leaves in the morning after the dew has evaporated and before the sun has had a chance to bring out the oils. Then, using a flat bottomed basket or box, place the leaves gently on the base in order to avoid bruising them and losing the essential oils, therefore, the flavour.

Pick only the amount you feel you can use in the near future. To simplify harvesting large quantities, it is recommended that you handle only one species at a time, to leave you time to pick over the harvest for badly blemished leaves, then to sort and tie the remainder into bunches, if necessary.

Leaves that will be eaten as salad greens — borage, burnet, nasturtiums, rocket, sorrel and winter savory — should be picked when young, before they flower, when they are at their most succulent.

Grassy-stalked leaves such as chives and parsley should be cut or pulled just above ground level. These salad herbs, which include angelica, are not suitable for drying and can be preserved by other means.

Aromatic evergreens such as rosemary, sage, savory and thyme have maximum flavour just before flowering. Basil, lovage, marjoram and mint have a sweeter flavour just before flowering. Using secateurs to

collect whole stems of these small-leaved herbs speeds up collection and makes drying more convenient.

If you wish to harvest the whole plant, perennials can be cut back to half the length of the year's growth; annuals can be cut to about 8 cm above the ground at the first harvest (early summer) and in autumn, to ground level.

Seed heads are ready for harvesting when they have lost their green colour and feel dry to the touch, preferably before they have scattered their seeds on the ground.

The seeds should be collected on a dry, warm day. Shake small seeds directly into a paper bag, or pop the heads or stems into bags, labelling and dating as you go. Remember to collect annual and culinary seeds for next year's propagation, let some such as dill and fennel self-sow, to ensure a crop next year.

Roots are best harvested in autumn. Annual roots are harvested when their growth cycle is complete, but perennial roots in their second or third year growth, when their active components, such as volatile oils or alkaloids, have developed. After digging up the root, take off what you require and replant the remainder to continue growing.

Most fleshy roots can be scrubbed clean, but others such as valerian should not be as they lose their active constituents.

Flowers are gathered as they fully open, the stalked varieties such as lavenders being snipped whole and the others picked carefully to avoid wilting or damage, especially if you wish to crystallise those such as violets and borage. Once picked, the flowers should be kept loose, not touching, in open containers to prevent sweating and bruising. Calendula petals are removed from the flowers to be dried and

stored, while other small-headed flowers such as chamomile are dried intact.

PRESERVING THE HARVEST

Leaves and flowers may now be dried in a variety of ways — by hanging them upside down in bunches in a warm, dry, dark area with some air movement, or by placing them on cloth frames or wire racks in such an area.

Dry strongly flavoured herbs such as lovage separately, away from other herbs, so that their flavours do not mingle. A loft, a sheltered garage ceiling or a hot water cupboard are all suitable places. If the drying area is dusty or if you are drying stems with seed heads, cover the bunches with brown paper bags loosely tied. These will act as dust covers and will catch seeds as they fall off stems or out of capsules.

Drying takes anywhere from five days to two weeks. Then your harvest is ready, it should be crisp and papery to the touch. A quicker method is to spread leaves on a muslin-covered rack in an oven which is set at a low temperature with the door open to let moisture escape.

Turn and stir the herbs until crisp. Small

quantities can be processed in a microwave oven, but although the flavour may not be affected, the therapeutic properties, such as those in chamomile, may be destroyed.

Roots should be cleaned, with fibrous parts removed, and cut into small, even portions or segments. Dry these in the oven at 120 to 140°C, turning them at intervals until they feel fragile and can be easily broken.

Leaves should be removed from stems and stored in labelled airtight, glass or plastic containers away from light, heat, moisture and contamination. Check them periodically for damp, mould and insects and discard them if these conditions occur. When properly dried, stored herbs will retain their freshness and flavour for at least a year.

Flowers, that have been dried the same way as leaves, are best stored spread out so that they maintain their shape, especially fragile flowers such as borage and violets.

Seeds for culinary use should be labelled and stored as leaves are, and seed for sowing should be kept in a cool, dark place free from frost.

Roots should also stored in airtight containers in a dark place. Those such as angelica and parsley may re-absorb air moisture. If this occurs and they become soft, discard them.

Other methods of preserving herbs include freezing, packing in vinegar or oil, and salt curing.

One of the most satisfying rewards for the herb grower is to present a friend, family member or neighbour with a generous bunch of fragrant, beautiful herbs, with the knowledge that they were carefully grown, tended and harvested by your own hand.

IDENTIFICATION AND PLANTING GUIDE

Abbreviations: A Annual; B Biennial; P Perennial; HP Herbaceous Perennial; WP Woody Perennial; Sp Spring; S Summer; A Autumn; W Winter; E Early; L Late

Herb	Habit	Propagation	Spacing	Comments
Agrimony (*Agrimonia eupatoria*)	P. Upright, compact, grows to 60 cm.	Seed—Sp Division—Sp and A	40 cm	Self-sows readily. Can become weedlike, but beautiful apricot scent.
All herb (*Coleus amboinicus*)	A. Fleshy leaves, thick stems. Sprawling plant, grows to 1 m.	Seed—Sp Cuttings—Sp	30 cm	Tropical plant, annual in temperate climate. Attractive pot plant.
Alpine strawberry (*Fragaria alpina*)	P. Clump-forming, compact, grows to 30 cm.	Seed—Sp and S Division—A	20 cm	Grows well in hanging baskets. Delicious strawberry fruit.
Angelica (*Angelica archangelica*)	B. Large leaves at base, flowering stalk, 2nd year grows to 1.5 m.	Fresh seed—A	1 m	Large but compact. Whole plant aromatic.
Anise (*Pimpinella anisum*)	A. Slender plant, grows to 50 cm.	Seed—Sp	20 cm	Long warm period needed to flower and set seed.
Anise hyssop (*Agastache foeniculum*)	P. Tall main stem, compact and upright, grows to 1 m.	Seed—Sp and A Cuttings—EA	30 cm	Short-lived bee plant. Long-lasting flowers.
Artemisia mugwort (*A. vulgaris*)	HP. Clump spreading to 1 m.	Seed—Sp Division—Sp	50 cm	Pungent and balsamic. Self-sows readily. Can become invasive.
Roman wormwood (*A. pontica*)	HP. Spreading clump, grows to 40 cm. Dies down in winter.	Division—Sp and A	40 cm	Deeply divided, grey, aromatic leaves. Keep trimmed.

Herb	Habit	Propagation	Spacing	Comments
tree wormwood (*A. arborescens*)	WP. Compact, large bush, grows to 80 cm.	Cuttings—Sp and A	80 cm	Good coastal hedge. Cut back S and A.
wormwood (*A. absinthum*)	HP. Upright, spreading, fernlike plant, grows to 1.5 m.	Seed—Sp Division—Sp and A	40 cm	Will keep animals from the garden. Cut after flowering.
Balm of Gilead (*Cedronella canariensis*)	WP. Camphor-scented, sprawling shrub, grows to 1 m.	Seed—Sp Cuttings—Sp and A	80 cm	Good bee plant. Prune regularly.
Basil				
bush basil (*O. minimum*)	A. Bright green bush, grows to 20 cm.	Seed—Sp	20 cm	As for sweet basil. Good container plant.
lettuce-leaf basil (*O. crispum*)	A. Crinkled, bright green, large leaves, grows to 50 cm.	Seed—Sp	40 cm	Needs protection from cold when young.
perennial basil (*Ocimum* spp.)	P. Green, compact bush, grows to 50 cm.	Seed—Sp	40 cm	Will not tolerate frosts or cold damp.
purple basil (*O. basilicum purpurescens*)	A. Similar to sweet basil but purple-leaved, grows to 50 cm.	Seed—Sp	30 cm	Needs protection from cold when young.
sacred basil (*O. sanctum*)	A. Soft, hairy, compact bush, grows to 30 cm.	Seed—Sp	30 cm	Needs protection from cold when young.
sweet basil (*Ocimum basilicum*)	A. Bright green bush, grows to 50 cm.	Seed—Sp	30 cm	Needs protection from cold, especially when young.
Bay (*Laurus nobilis*)	Compact shrub or tree, grows to 20 m when mature.	Seed—Sp Cuttings—Sp and A	1 m	Slow-growing. Good pot or lawn specimen or pruned as hedge.
Bergamot (*Monarda didyma*)	HP. Spreading clump with flowers. Grows to 60 cm.	Seed—Sp Division—Sp and A	40 cm	Needs protection from frost. Cut back in A. Good bee plant.

Herb	Habit	Propagation	Spacing	Comments
Betony (*Stachys officinalis*)	P. Compact clump with flowers, grows to 60 cm.	Seed—Sp Division—Sp and A	40 cm	Likes semi-shade. Cut off old growth. Flowers S and A.
Borage (*Borago officinalis*)	A. Most tolerant plant, grows to 1 m.	Seed—Sp and A	1 m	Bees love its blue flowers. Self-sows freely.
Bugle (*Ajuga reptans*)	P. Low-spreading, tolerant plant with flowers, grows to 15 cm.	Seed—Sp Division—Sp and A	20 cm	Grows well in pots. Good ground cover and rockery plant.
Calendula (pot marigold— *C. officinalis*)	A. Sprawling, bushy habit, grows to 50 cm.	Seed—Sp Division—Sp and A	50 cm	Cut back regularly for constant flowering. Self-sows readily. Will grow in poor soils.
Caraway (*Carum carvi*)	A/B (depends on when seed is sown). Slender plant, grows in clump to 50 cm.	Seed—Sp and A	40 cm	Will rot in winter if drainage is poor. Seeds used in bread making.
Catmint (*Nepeta mussinii*)	P. Low, bushy growth with flowers, grows to 20 cm. Dies down in W.	Seed—Sp Division—Sp and A	50 cm	Ornamental form of catnip. Perfect foil for roses and borders.
Catnip (*Nepeta cataria*)	P. Strong stems grow to 1–2 m. Dies down in winter.	Seed—Sp Division—Sp and A	30 cm	Cats drool over it. Protect young plants.
Chamomile German chamomile (*Matricaria chamomila*)	A. Flowering stems grow to 30 cm.	Seed—Sp and A	15 cm	The dried flowers make excellent tea. Likes sun.
Roman chamomile (*Anthemis nobilis*)	P. Low, spreading plant with trailing stems, grows to 15 cm.	Seed—Sp Division—Sp and A	15 cm	Beautifully scented herb for lawn, seat, path or bank. Prefers sandy soil.

Herb	Habit	Propagation	Spacing	Comments
Chervil (*Anthriscus cerefolium*)	A. Compact, fernlike, bright green plant, grows to 80 cm.	Seed—Sp and A	20 cm	Self-sows readily. Likes cool spots. Good under deciduous trees.
Chives (*Allium schoenoprasum*)	HP. Clumps of shoots from bulbs grow to 20–50 cm. Dies back in winter.	Seed—Sp and S Bulb division—S and A	20 cm	Lift and divide every 2 years. Good edging and pot plant.
garlic chives (*A. tuberosum*)	HP. Less dense clump than chives. Grows to 30–50 cm.	As for chives	20 cm	As for chives.
Comfrey (*Symphytum officinalis*)	P. Vigorous, upright plant, grows to 1.5 m.	Division—Sp	70 cm	Needs to be contained. Plant out in permanent position.
Coriander (*Coriandrum sativum*)	A. Delicate shrublike plant, grows to 50 cm.	Seed—Sp and A	20 cm	Will self-sow. Unusual pungent scent.
Costmary (*Chrysanthemum balsamita*)	P. Sprawling, rooted clump with flowering stem to 1.5 m.	Division—Sp and A	60 cm	Very old cultivar, also known as alecost and bible leaf.
Curry plant (*Helichrysum angustifolium*)	P. Low, silvery bush with flower heads to 20 cm.	Stem cuttings—Sp and A	30 cm	Prune lightly ESp and A. Good edging and border plant.
Dill (*Anethum graveolens*)	A. Tall, feathery plant, grows to 80 cm.	Seed—Sp, S and A	70 cm	Needs some wind protection.
Feverfew (*Chrysanthemum parthenium*)	WP. Bright green, tolerant plant, grows to 70 cm.	Seed—Sp and A Cuttings—Sp Division—Sp	40 cm	Self-sows readily. Cut back after flowering.
Horehound (*Marrubium vulgare*)	HP. Silvery, bushy growth to 50 cm.	Seed—LSp Division—Sp Cuttings—S	30 cm	Some wind protection needed. Prune in Sp to prevent woodiness.
Hyssop (*Hyssopus officinalis*)	WP. Hardy, bushy shrub, grows to 40 cm.	Seed—Sp Cuttings—Sp Division—A	40 cm	Cut back in A. Good low hedge or border plant to attract bees and butterflies.

Herb	Habit	Propagation	Spacing	Comments
Lady's bedstraw (*Galium verum*)	P. Hardy, honey-scented, delicate plant, grows to 15 cm.	Seed—S Division—Sp and A	40 cm	Attractive and useful ground cover. A dyer's plant.
Lavender English lavender (*Lavandula angustifolia*)	WP. Bushy, compact, grey shrub, grows to 80 cm. Dwarf forms available.	Seed—Sp Cuttings—Sp and A	40 cm	Beautiful hedge or specimen. Cut back after flowering.
French lavender (*L. dentata*)	WP. Bushy, compact, grey shrub with toothed leaves. Grows to 1 m.	As for English lavender	60 cm	Good medium-sized hedge plant. Flowers most of the year.
green lavender (*L. viridis*)	WP. Green-foliaged, compact shrub with distinct scent. Grows to 60 cm.	As for English lavender	40 cm	Cut back in A. Soil must be well drained.
Lemon balm (*Melissa officinalis*)	P. Bright green, tolerant shrub, grows in clump to 2 m.	Seed—Sp and A Division—Sp and A	60 cm	Cut back after flowering. Self-sows easily.
Lemon verbena (*Lippia citriodora*)	P. Deciduous shrub, grows to 2.5 m when mature.	Seed—Sp Softwood cuttings—Sp	1 m	Needs some shelter when young and is frost tender.
Lovage (*Levisticum officinale*)	HP. Vigorous, tall stalks to 2 m.	Seed—Sp and A Division—Sp and A	60 cm	A stately, strongly aromatic plant. Good background specimen.
Marjoram golden marjoram (*Origanum majorana*)	WP. Golden, low-creeping bush. May die back in winter.	Seed—Sp Division—Sp and A	30 cm	Striking ground cover. Good in tubs.
pot marjoram (*O. onites*)	HP. Grows to 50 cm. Bushy habit. Dies back in W.	Seed—Sp Division—LSp	40 cm	Hardy form with robust flavour.

Herb	Habit	Propagation	Spacing	Comments
sweet marjoram (*Majorana hortensis*)	WP. Small grey-green bush, grows to 30–50 cm. Grown as annual.	Seed—Sp Cuttings—A Division—A	30 cm	Best form for culinary use.
wild marjoram (*O. vulgare*)	HP. Forms dense mat with flowering stems to 60 cm.	Seed—Sp Division—LSp	40 cm	Often called oregano. The least aromatic of all.
Mint (*Mentha* spp.) applemint (*M. suaveolens*)	HP. Vigorous, spreading clump with soft, green, downy leaves.	Seed—Sp Division—Sp	50 cm	Needs to be contained. Looks good in large pots.
eau de cologne mint (*M.* × *piperita* 'Citrata')	P. Wine and green stems. Flowering to 1 m. Dies back in winter.	Division—Sp and S	50 cm	Lovely fresh scent. Can become invasive so needs to be contained.
pennyroyal (*M. pulegium*)	P. A vigorous, spreading clump with flowers, grows to 20–30 cm.	Seed—Sp Division—Sp and A	30 cm	Good ground cover. Can be used for lawn.
peppermint (*M. piperita*)	P. Vigorous, spreading clump flowering to 60 cm. W dormant.	Seed—Sp Division—Sp and S	50 cm	Old culinary favourite. Needs to be contained.
spearmint (*M. spicata*)	HP. Creeping rootstock. Grows to 1 m in flower. Dies down in W.	As for peppermint	30 cm	Best culinary mint.
Parsley (*Petroselinum* spp.) curly-leaf parsley (*P. crispum*)	B. Compact clump, grows to 60 cm. Dark green leaves.	Seed—Sp and A	40 cm	Milder flavour than plain-leaf parsley. Germination takes 4–6 weeks.

Herb	Habit	Propagation	Spacing	Comments
plain-leaf parsley (*P. neopolitanum*)	B. Compact clump, grows to 70 cm. Dark green, divided leaves.	As for curly-leaf parsley	50 cm	Very hardy, strong-flavoured, culinary herb. Self-sows.
Rocket (*Eruca sativa*)	A. Quick-growing salad herb. Grows to 30–70 cm.	Seed—Sp and S	20 cm	Self-sows readily. Harvest young leaves regularly.
Rosemary (*Rosmarinus officinalis*)	WP. Sprawling, woody shrub, grows to 50 cm.	Seed—Sp Cuttings—Sp and A	60 cm	Good hedge plant. Keep trimmed for shape. Prefers limy soil.
prostrate rosemary (*R. prostrata*)	WP. Trailing creeper, grows to 15 cm.	Seed—Sp Cuttings—Sp and A Layering—Sp, S and A	40 cm	Good hardy ground cover. Used in rockeries, hanging containers. Slow to germinate.
Rue (*Ruta graveolens*)	P. Tolerant, pungent, blue-green, compact bush, grows to 1 m.	Seed—Sp Cuttings—Sp and S	50 cm	Prefers dry soil.
Sage (*Salvia officinalis*)	WP. Short-lived, bushy, compact shrub, grows to 80 cm.	Seed—Sp Cuttings—Sp and A Layering—Sp and S	40 cm	Many cultivars with various leaf and flower colours. Broad-leaf does not flower.
clary sage (*S. sclarea*)	B. Tall, sprawling clump, grows to 1 m.	Seed—Sp and A	60 cm	An ornamental that needs lots of space.
pineapple sage (*S. rutilans*)	WP. Stems to 1 m and red flowers all winter.	Cuttings—Sp and A Division—Sp	60 cm	Frost sensitive. Cut back LW. Bees love it.
Salad burnet (*Sanguisorba minor*)	P. Dainty, leafy clump, grows to 20–25 cm. Flowering stalks to 50 cm.	Seed—Sp and A	40 cm	Useful low border plant. Grows well in W.

IDENTIFICATION AND PLANTING GUIDE

Herb	Habit	Propagation	Spacing	Comments
Santolina (lavender cotton— *S. chamaecyparissus*)	WP. Coral-like, grey, scented, compact bush, grows to 45 cm.	Seed—Sp Cuttings—Sp and A	30 cm	Trim after flowering. Good low hedge, contrast and rockery plant.
Savory summer savory (*Satureja hortensis*)	A. Green-red, compact bush, grows to 25–40 cm.	Seed—Sp	30 cm	Sow successively for continuous harvesting.
winter savory (*S. montana*)	WP. Low, straggly bush. Also in prostrate form.	Cuttings—Sp and A Layering—Sp	40 cm	Cut back after flowering.
Sweet cicely (*Myrrhis odorata*)	HP. Soft, green, fernlike stems growing to 80 cm.	Seed—A Division—A	50 cm	Slow to germinate.
Tansy (*Tanacetum vulgare*)	HP. Dark green, vigorous, spreading clump, grows to 90 cm. Can rampage.	Division—Sp and A	70 cm	Very hardy. Keep under strict control. Good compost plant.
Tarragon French tarragon (*Artemisia dracunculus*)	HP. Bright green, spreading plant, grows to 40 cm.	Division—Sp	30 cm	Dig and replant every 2–3 years. Needs frost protection.
Thyme (*Thymus vulgaris*)	WP. Dark green, aromatic, compact bush growing to 30 cm.	Seed—Sp Layering—Sp, S and A Division—Sp	30 cm	Good low hedge or border plant. Trim after flowering.
caraway thyme (*T. herba barona*)	WP. Green, spreading ground cover, grows to 5 cm.	As for thyme	30 cm	Good ground cover for dry areas.
lemon thyme (*T. citriodorus*)	P. Green, spreading shrub, grows to 20 cm.	As for thyme	30 cm	Silver and gold varieties. Good for rockeries and borders.

Herb	Habit	Propagation	Spacing	Comments
orange thyme (*T. fragrantissimum*)	P. Blue-grey, straggly, spreading bush. Grows to 30 cm.	Seed—Sp Cuttings—Sp and A	20 cm	Keep trimmed.
wild thyme (*T. serpyllum*)	P. Matting ground cover growing from 3–20 cm high.	Seed—Sp Division—Sp and A	30 cm	Excellent hardy ground cover and lawn plant.
Valerian (*Valeriana officinalis*)	P. Tolerant, spreading, light green clump, grows to 1 m or more.	Seed—Sp Division—Sp and A	60 cm	Lovely back of border plant. Flowers in second year.
Vervain (*Verbena officinalis*)	P. Dark green, leafy clump, grows to 80 cm. Dies back in W.	Seed—Sp (erratic germination)	30 cm	Old cultivar. Cut back in W.
Weld (*Reseda luteola*)	B. Low rosette in 1st year. Flowering spikes to 1 m in 2nd year.	Seed—Sp	50 cm	A dyer's plant. Good back of border plant.
Woad (*Isatis tinctoria*)	B. Blue-green clump in 1st year. Flowering stalk to 1 m in 2nd year.	Seed—Sp	50 cm	Unusual flat, black, papery pods. A dyer's plant. Good back of border plant.
Woodruff (*Galium odoratum*)	P. Spreading, bright green plant growing to 30 cm.	Seed—LS Division—S	20 cm	Germination may take 12 months. Will not grow in hot, dry conditions.
Yarrow (*Achillea millefolium*)	P. Low, spreading, feathery, green clump with flowers to 1 m.	Seed—Sp Division—Sp and A	50 cm	Can be invasive. Good ground cover in wild areas.
sneezewort (*A. ptarmica*)	P. Spreading, leafy clump with flowering stems to 50 cm.	As for yarrow	30 cm	Ornamental and easy to grow.

INDEX

The page numbers in **bold** type indicate illustrations.

47

CONCILIUM
Religion in the Seventies

CONCILIUM

Religion in the Seventies

Volume 67: Church History

HISTORY

SELF-UNDERSTANDING
OF THE CHURCH

Edited by

Roger Aubert

Herder and Herder

1971
HERDER AND HERDER NEW YORK
232 Madison Avenue, New York 10016

CONTENTS

PART II
BULLETINS

Editorial

IN his article entitled *"Kirchengeschichte"* in the *Lexikon für Theologie und Kirche* Hubert Jedin has briefly pointed out just how much the idea of the Church with which an historian implicitly or explicitly operates is a crucial factor in determining the object and the task of Church history as an intellectual discipline. Jedin reveals his own standpoint to be that the object of Church history is "the realization of the essential nature of the Church in time and space"—leaving it to theology to settle what the essential nature of the Church is; just as "its founding by Jesus Christ and its essential identity within the forms of its historical manifestation" are presupposed as theologically "given" factors in historical inquiry, and in a description of the Church's various phases of development. The three theological presuppositions cannot be contained in a-historical formulas: theology itself has a history; and if the three above-mentioned tenets are at the centre of interest, they are there because of a new spate of questioning in a new historico-social situation. The Church historian is walking with his eyes shut if he refuses to admit reflection on these theological assumptions into his own line of business; but on the other hand he cannot wait for a settled verdict before starting on his journey.

It is better that alongside or inside the discussion about the nature of the Church he should make his own typically historical contribution at greater depth. A profane theory of history, starting from the peculiar character of historical thinking, which is basically developmental or evolutionary, postulates that

7

the nature of man and of all his social constructions is involved in a multiform, evolutionary process, a process of *becoming*, and is not merely the explication of an implicit, a-historical nature. That *becoming* does not mean that there are no phases in which the sense of identity may be paramount: a closed society with an explicitly received ideology may have such a sure and clear-cut idea of itself that the understanding of this historical self may assume the colouring of a metaphysically timeless proposition concerning the immutable nature of men and of human constructions. The historian will not express himself as to the value or otherwise of metaphysical pronouncements: he confines himself to elucidating the phases of development in human history and giving a clearly outlined answer to the question: How have men in various societies understood themselves and their community? What, individually and collectively, was their self-understanding?

Jedin recognizes that "searching for the historically evolving self-understanding (*Selbstverständnis*) of men-in-society" is also a very fruitful way of talking about and defining the task of the scientifically disciplined Church historian. Ernst Benz had earlier defined Church history as the *"Selbstverständnis der Kirche"*—the Church's self-understanding—and Jedin worked out in brief how the writing of Church history might be made to contribute in particular to the process whereby the Church as a community comes to consciousness: "The story of the Church is one of development from an unreflective being in the Church to a conscious grasp of the Church as an historical entity with the methods of history as a discipline. The development of Church history depends just as much, therefore, on the Church's self-understanding as on the cultivation and refining of historical criticism."

In the 1970 Church history issue of *Concilium* some attention was given to the above-mentioned aspect: developments in historical method, specifically in the context of the developments in the modern human and social sciences. This time we wanted to see closer attention given to the successive phases in the development of the understanding the Church has had of itself, so that on the basis of these historical researches the Church as an historical entity might be set in a clearer light: it is a question of different phases in the "history of the Church's self-understanding".

From the standpoint of theology and of the theory of history, such an undertaking is not without its problems. That there are various phases in the historical self-understanding of the Church is not to be doubted. Our whole style of living today is making inescapably obvious the social and psychological phenomenon of change in the self-consciousness of the Catholic community— change that is affecting large groups of people. It would serve no purpose to deny that the notion of the Church as the people of God "on the move", which many in various quarters have come to share, thanks to the work of Vatican II, evinces a socio-psychological awareness plainly different from what, to judge from the ecclesiastical writings of the time, was current in the post-Tridentine Church. But when that evolution has been identified and acknowledged, there still persists, of course, the theological problem of the essential identity of this Church, running through the various forms of its historical manifestation, which Jedin was speaking about. A second difficulty is this: the historical evolution of the Church's self-understanding has not been straightforward. Substantial groups in what was initially the one Church have split off into separate institutions; *within* each of these distinct churches there are typifying differences with regard to what is and was seen as the essential nature or being of the Church. Sectarian groups on the Left and on the Right have each given the self-understanding of the Church their own particular emphasis.

In view of all this, the question inevitably arises: What then is this Church, whose self-understanding we keep talking about? Who or what is said to "understand itself"? Does there exist a Church above and beyond the churches, ecclesial groups and individual believers? A Church which is able to comprehend and express itself as a totality, so that all the members recognize themselves in that self-expression, are able to endorse it, and thus turn it into authentic self-understanding? If so, then what or who is the organ that formulates this self-understanding, that self-expression? Is it the pope, a council, the congregation at prayer, theologians...? To this question also, whether from the historical or the theological side, a variable answer can be given.

We can best approach this whole problematical area by means of an example. Medieval theologians and canonists gave ample thought to this matter, knew the doctrine of the Church as the mystical body of Christ, but elaborated upon it, especially in the fourteenth and fifteenth centuries, with reference to the Church as a legal institution, *corpus juridicum, corpus politicum*; and so the most important issues came to be those concerned with the position of pope and council vis-à-vis the community of believers, with a view to juridical procedures regarding faith, church unity and reform. The answers were far from being homogeneous: in defining that position, papalists and conciliarists were miles apart; and between the conciliarists of Constance and Basle there were again differences of outlook. When nowadays an historian examines this multiplicity of opinions in the light of the whole political and social context of that time, a lot of these theories turn out to be reflections of political theories about the relationship between people, representative assembly and government at the top. The model of the Italian city state, in particular, would seem to have had a profound influence. Without wanting to pronounce on the theological validity of the various standpoints, historical inquiry serves to confirm that through its theologians and canonists the Church of that time likewise understood itself in terms of the actual socio-juridical state of affairs all around it.

To an historian this conclusion is really very obvious; so much so, in fact, that he recognizes here a sociological problem calling in a general sense for elucidation: man evidently understands the society planned by him as a function of the proposed ends and the chosen means of realizing a greater measure of humanity; and the system functioning in this way again determines man's understanding of himself. The Church's self-understanding is embedded in this process.

We therefore wanted to begin this number with a sociological consideration of the role the historian can play in the process within the Church by which it attains to awareness. In the closing article it is again a sociologist who tries to indicate what are the general factors determining the Church's self-understanding now. In between these two articles will be found some discussion of the Church community's self-understanding in different periods of the history of that community. These historians are thereby fulfilling a role in the growth of the community to consciousness now. But anyone reading this number cannot but be aware of what is implied by the fact that the discussion here is conducted by *historians*, with not a theologian among them.

Much to the point here is the introductory analysis by E. Poulat, which follows aptly upon the analysis of problems relating to methods in Church history, given in the 1970 Church history number of *Concilium*.

Poulat analyses the term "self-understanding" and its content, and finds that in this context Church history is a function of the lived consciousness of the Church, but also that however much one may aspire to objectivity the articulation of this consciousness is inextricably tangled up with all sorts of personal and social subjective factors. He reflects on the historians' role in the process of bringing to consciousness the Church, which thanks to them is beginning to become aware of the depth of its historical determination and its cultural plasticity. But he also points out the difference in role between the historian and the theologian and the profound range of problems bound up with this articulation of the Church's self-understanding: the historian takes note of the many different modes of understanding that exist, whereas the theologian was and is inclined to make a selection and exhibit one of them as being "right", or even to dogmatize: the *ecclesia primitiva* has long fulfilled the role of an ideal—likewise the Church of the Middle Ages and its synthesis of faith and knowledge. A theological finding of this sort is then held up to the historian as a valid yardstick for historical judgment too. Next: If the business of "self-understanding" is already difficult enough at the individual human level, contemporary theology, because of its more and more intense contacts with the human and social sciences, has arrived at a more relative position vis-à-vis excessively traditionalist views of the Church; but at the same time modern theology has been forced by all this to realize to what an extent psychological and sociological principles condition the process of self-understanding in man and society, even within the Church itself. And that exposes a third difficulty: How much the more is all this bound to apply when the task is to dig down to and articulate the self-understanding of the Church in bygone centuries, from which the modern historian is made so very remote by the major cultural changes of our own day.

In the earlier number (1970) it was pointed out that so-called critical theories, particularly in the social sciences, try here and there to put in operation what is supposed to be a critical science of history in which a normative mode of thinking, based on this or that interpretation of life, threatens to absorb scientific objectivity. For Church history, too, that confusion between a theological mode of thinking, which both engenders norms and is conditioned by them, and strictly scientific historical inquiry and historiography, is a very real thing: can the historian *qua* historian gauge to what extent a particular historical self-understanding of the Church, say, that of the Church of the Renaissance and the Baroque period, tallies with what according to the theologians "*the* Church" *has* to be? Ideally, one might argue as follows: As long as an ecclesial community is *unanimous* in its self-understanding—as that is expressed by its leaders, theologians, preachers, writers, and so on—the Church historian should be able to take that unanimously received self-understanding as a yardstick for gauging the past. But it is obvious that in actual fact this self-understanding in every society, the Church included, is *always pluriform*, the moment one gets down to concrete details; and in a way pluriformity rules out unanimity. What then is in fact the historian's role? He is left with no other possibility than that of scientific, "norm-free" analysis, and of describing, as objectively as he can, the "actual situation". But he is aware of all the hermeneutical problems *and* of the critique of them provided on the basis of the new critical theory....

Editorially, the standpoint we adopt in this number is that the historian can only place on record the many forms of self-understanding as they find expression in the various modes of theologizing: namely, in ecclesiology, in prayer and devotion, in the activity of the Church at all levels of man's life. In making comparisons, he can keep a look-out for constant elements that will show in what ways the historical, evolving Church has remained consistent; yet will he find more than the indeed constantly repeated confession of belief: Jesus is Lord, and the gathering of the congregation in the celebration of the Eucharist? But even that reiterated confession would seem to be the object of unceasing hermeneutics, as a function of the ever-changing contemporary self-understanding of the faithful. And the evolution of thinking about what the eucharistic meal could and should signify is still very much on the move. Can the historian do more than confirm that time and again there have been people who in their own way have echoed the words of Peter: *Thou hast the words of eternal life*, but that they have always kept trying to give these words form and shape in *time-bound*, historical, ephemeral interpretations?

Here a number of historians offer to put into words what they have recognized to be the Church's self-understanding at a particular time, in this or that cultural milieu. It proved to be no simple task; and it usually demanded more than the maximum number of words allowed. For that reason, alas, we eventually found ourselves obliged to look elsewhere for a place to accommodate the excellent article by A. Dupront: *De l'Eglise aux temps modernes*. The interested reader will find his article, which properly belongs to this series, in the current or prospective volume of the *Revue d'Histoire ecclésiastique*.

Evident from the articles included here—as well as from Dupront's—is the plurality, both diachronic and synchronic, of the self-understanding of the Church, and also the diversity of levels at which this self-understanding occurs. A great deal of the prevailing divergence among the churches rests on these differences in self-understanding, differences that are bound up to a considerable extent with a differing evaluation of certain historical forms of the Church's life. The theological question thrown up by the historical analysis is therefore whether that diversity can exist within a single model of Catholicism, or whether it is a matter of differing models in conflict with one another. The very term "Church", so long as it is general and indeterminate, confronts the historian with the question of the concept's univocity and instrumentality. Perhaps the historian should devise a special language as a function of the methodological requirements engendered by this object. At any rate, he cannot simply go on using the language of his sources, whilst leaving its reinterpretation on the lines of an up--to-date understanding of the Church's past to anyone, believer or unbeliever, who wants to dig into it. If he were to do that, he would be failing to act in his role of interpreter of the lived consciousness of the Church, and would be recoiling from a notion of his task that asks him, for the benefit of that same Church, to say in so many (ephemeral) words how, in his view, the Church has seen itself as an historical phenomenon, especially in its relation to the history of that human race to whom it is for the Church to proclaim throughout all ages that Jesus Christ is Lord.

ANTON WEILER

Translated by Hubert Hoskins

PART I
ARTICLES

Emile Poulat

History and the Church: A Mutual View

THE best thing that can happen to a neatly turned formula is for it to enter the public domain and gain the sort of currency there that cuts it off completely from its original function. Everyone uses it for his own ends and reads his own meaning into it; gradually it takes on the ballast of all the commentaries that come to be made on it. It is not, like a scientific conclusion, the finished expression of a theoretical consensus or the result of a series of experiments, but the intuitive and initial answer to a question which at a given moment is felt more or less clearly to be important: it illumines in a new way a certain debate, which tends to react to the novel stimulus by taking off in various new directions. Ranke, Marx and Weber are prime examples in this regard: their influence would surely have been less extensive if their work had attracted a smaller number of commentaries and less discussion.[1] This is a fascinating phenomenon for the historian, who is too often fated to languish in the limbo of polemical discussions which add nothing to what is already known and advanced. In scientific disciplines, in their foremost areas in fact, one can find the same array that is so familiar to the Church historian: the initiator, the group, a certain development, orthodoxy, variations, even hermeneutics.

Representing the history of the Church as the Church's "self-understanding" is to use one of these synthetic formulas which can lead astray as well as stimulate thought, and which tend to

[1] For Max Weber, see Philippe Besnard, *Capitalisme et protestantisme* (Paris, 1970).

17

attract a whole range of interpretations. To intervene in this particular debate is to add another response to a whole collection of
them. The historian cannot restrict his examination of the formula to the exact context of its first use; he must refer to other
possible contexts.

The function of history is to understand; but one does not
"self-understand" something outside oneself. At most one understands it by reference to oneself, by reference to what one is and
to what one does. A formulary approach in the case in point implies that there is no real externality. Firstly, the historiography
of the Church would seem to be viewed as a function of the ex-
periential consciousness of the Church; as if it were part of it
in the sense of being carried along in its ever-flowing current.
Secondly, the Church historian shares in this lived consciousness
which places him within the fold of the faithful people of God
—a believer among the believers. From history-as-life to history-as-
science, the continuity is affirmed as if it were a matter of course.

In the end, the formula in question appears as the Christian
historian's justification or the rationalization of his work and
motives. From this viewpoint, it is true, legitimate, well-grounded
and wholly established, and there is no need to set a different
idea against it. Yet it is possible that it does not proficiently take
into account the real work of history as it is manifested in our
society, and in its pluralistic aspects; or, indeed, the consequences
which this work has for the Church's own understanding—the
unforeseen feedback effect.

I happen to be writing these observations during a stay in
Quebec. Here the religious situation is rapidly changing. Historical research helps along this process of development at the
same time as it is itself subject to it: it is an interactive process.
But in fact the work of historical revision began well before the
present religious ferment became so spectacular. "One of the
best-established and most widespread images of French Canada
is that of its religious homogeneity. If one thinks of French
Canada, one immediately thinks of an essentially Catholic community, attached to its faith, submissive to its pastors, respecting
all that emanates from Rome, and devoted to the missionary
apostolate. . . . We have entertained, affirmed and proclaimed
this conception of ourselves both at home and abroad. . . . Yet

this idea of the religious unity of French Canada is a recent one . . . and would seem to have crystallized only at the end of the last century. . . . Religious conflicts rather than religious unity would seem to have been the dominant factor of the nineteenth century as far as French-Canadian Catholicism was concerned."[2] In 1908, however, one bishop of Quebec did not scruple to proclaim, in France, that "French Canada has no history". It was this deficiency—or rather ignorance—which was to determine the vocation of Father Lionel Groulx, who was given a chair by the University of Montreal for this purpose in 1915.[3]

The example suits the case. All the problems are there, inextricably mingled one with the other. At first, history wants to help recreate a collective memory which proved deficient, and whose loss brought about a crisis of identity—at the risk, indeed, of ethno-religious assimilation by the adjacent English-speaking, Protestant culture. And then history tries to attack this celebration with its loading of myth and ideology, in order to rediscover more accurately the features of the past reality. But in neither case is history merely a science—it is also a form of passionate enthusiasm. In both cases it renews its understanding under the effect of non-historical factors: on the one hand, a complex of problems connected with the evolution of a particular society, which supplies the historian with questions; on the other hand, an axiomatic system, which makes him adopt a scale of values on which to base his judgments. If Father Groulx seemed deserving of criticism to a new generation, it is not basically because he was not a wholly expert practitioner of his calling (it would be unjust and anachronistic to attack him on that ground), and was therefore more exacting; it is because the way of looking at men and events has changed in the meantime, for reasons which would seem hardly to be due to historical studies. Very often history, far from being determinative, is content to follow. For this very reason it is not a luxury; nowadays it seems to us more a servant than a master—whatever its dreams of independence might be. Whether it is a question of those who write or those who write about history, at all levels the objectivity of the method

[2] Fernand Dumont and Guy Rocher, in *Le Canada français aujourd'hui et demain* (Paris, 1961), pp. 24–5.
[3] Lionel Groulx, *Mes Mémoires* (Montreal, 1970), vol. 1, pp. 173–4.

appears as something that cannot be dissociated from a social fabric composed of many different forms of subjectivity.

Such is the fundamental problem for the historian reflecting on his profession. But let us return to the example put forward above—the *unified ideology* of French Canada (one race, and one faith). At the start this is no more than an orientation for research; in the end it is a methodically structured object whose consistency has been tested, limits defined, importance appreciated, and reasons discovered, and so on. Far from adhering tenaciously to the convictions of the dominant group and to its leaders' affirmations, the historian will have given free rein to his professional curiosity. Throughout his inquiry, he will have had only one preoccupation: to approach this *fact* in order to understand and explain it: i.e., simultaneously to elucidate its structure and integrate it in a larger historical construct or constructs.

But has anyone ever come across this "pure historian" wholly taken up by a quest for an ideal objectivity? Even if he were a possibility, should he be the recommended norm? In addition to decluding himself, surely an historian with such pretensions would be failing in his human duty of commitment and alignment. For a group it is not just a question of facts, but of values. Groups tend to confront themselves in order to evaluate, and stabilize the value of, the same facts; and to qualify them differently. Groulx set a value on a unified ideology and tended to put a null value on, or evaluate as bad, anything which seemed to oppose it. His successors have tended to take the contrary view, or to revive currents of thought that were formerly opposed or suppressed.

Of course this committed attitude on the part of the historian has a double effect: on the one hand, it forces him to enter an area that was previously deserted, because it requires the justification or additional tricking out of a collective behaviour, of a group cause; but on the other hand, it endows this area with a certain degree of privilege to the disadvantage of other abandoned or obscured sectors. Doesn't this put us in an impasse? In one sense, it does, since we have to accept that the historian and the history he writes are immersed in the history which is being made; if he seeks to abstain from the common enterprise

in order (as he thinks) the better to devote himself to his scholarly
or scientific research, will he really be able to escape the history
that has made him and which moulds him every day of his life?
But this is really a vain debate, which would be profitless if it
were not already inadequate in its premisses. It is a rejection that
the historian has to oppose from the start and definitively: not
just a rejection of "values", of "commitment", under the pretext
of scientific purity, but of the unceasing movement (which is
often unconscious) from one history to another. Each history en-
joys its own specific nature, and the inner duality experienced
by the historian need not force him into either a state of confusion or an attitude of withdrawal, but to distinguish roles and
levels.

It is not a question of indifferentism, which sees everything
as an "equally best" of all possible things, but of a refusal to
approximate facts to an *a priori* privileged system of values, and
one which is carefully withdrawn from history. In other words,
the historian must avoid any attitude which would limit the field
of his research. At present there is much talk of ecumenism: the
historian has to acknowledge that it is far from being a phenomenon that can merely be reduced to the condition of its major
and best-known organizational forms, or be neatly encompassed
by the unilateral theological certainties of the associated ideology.
And he has to search his mind and conscience in regard to the
new values by which the young generation are so fired when they
support an ecumenism which appears to protest against the tardy
progress and dogmatisms of established mechanisms. As soon as
he thinks this way, whether he likes it or no, he is beginning to
take part in the most burning of contemporary debates without
necessarily being party to them in person.

History as a science is militant by virtue of the sole fact that it
is a science and that it is historical science. There is absolutely no
need for it to search for a cause or a master. Its utility is clear to
the extent to which it obeys its nature, rather than in trying to
accord with the requirements placed upon it from outside. Why
should commitment not be understood in the terms of organized
militancy? Religious history has done a lot of work in the last
century; it is no longer a programme, but what has been the
price of its coming to stay? In fact it has seemed more of an

obstacle than a precious helper, and its usefulness today is certainly not what was expected from it: it is there—a result which has to be taken into account in the calculation, and one which makes considerable revisions necessary. Delicate problems of deontology are involved here, because in the long run it is always subject to the temptation to make itself useful or to let itself be used.

Struggles for History is the title of a Festschrift for Lucien Febvre. And it is as a struggle for the sake of history that the work of Church historians since Duchesne, the Bollandists and a great number of exegetes may be seen. They could not afford to deviate from this course, even under the pretext of serving a Church which today—thanks to them (and this is the unforeseen though fundamental increment)—is beginning to become aware of the full extent of its historical conditioning and its cultural plasticity: not only in its institutional forms, but even in its language, and in its formulations and modes of thought. Undoubtedly this self-reconsideration of the Church undertaken at the suit of its historians can be assessed as much more important than all the chapters of its history now under revision.

In the first place, this implies that even if no one is obliged to be an historian, it is not by being the Church's man that the historian can best serve his Church, but by being a scholar and a scientist as rigorously as the discipline requires. Of course that is not an easy path to take. Happy the man who is fully integrated and at peace with himself. More often, like Jacob who was never finished with his wrestling with the angel in the night, he will experience the fruitful though insoluble tension of an inner duality between the ideal of critical objectivity and the social subjectivity of his adherence. Since he cannot escape this situation, he has to do his possible best: not only in following the advice of his spiritual superiors, but in resorting to the devices of the human sciences.

In the second place, it means that I wholly share the opinions and positions of Giuseppe Alberigo expressed in the last number of *Concilium* concerned with this subject:[4] "Church history is and must remain an historical discipline"; it can in no way be

[4] G. Alberigo, "New Frontiers in Church History", *Concilium*, vol. 7, 6, pp. 68–84 (American edn., vol. 57).

qualified as a theological discipline, and in no way can one allow theology to assume the task of deciding its object. Consequently, Church history is dependent on a variety of *non-religious* certainty, in the same way as all the "religious sciences"—allowing this term the same wholly secular meaning which it had when, in 1886, the religious sciences replaced the old Faculty of theology at the Sorbonne.[5] Despite the considerable number of Catholic scholars who see no difficulty in adopting this position, there is one point involved in it which remains no less delicate—that of the relation between the history of Christian origins and biblical exegesis. To the extent to which exegesis seems to think of itself more and more as a theological discipline (whereas at the beginning of this century it took up the stance of an historical discipline in regard to theology), the whole problem has to be reconsidered on the basis of a new and more profound analysis which will allow a precise distinction to be made between the objects concerned. Everyone would gain from such a fundamental reassessment.

Somewhat analogously, it is certain that one of the problems of the moment is the attention paid to history by theologians. It is a proof of its success, but also a source of derivative endeavours. A master of theology can be a great historian—but that does not mean that the two disciplines do not have jealously to preserve their autonomy. Think of the number of theological treatises one sees these days in which "theology" appears only as a final reflection (quite often hastily tacked on) on an "historical" datum presented neither with clear and well-defined terms nor with an unambiguous methodology. On the other hand, think of the number of history dons who willingly accept, as an appropriate conceptual framework, theological elaborations which seem to them essential, or at least allow their work to be contaminated by a language or interpretations which really demand much more preliminary criticism. Perhaps one should recall the fact that the "people of God", which has become so popular a reference point among theologians since Vatican II,

[5] See E. & O. Poulat, "Le Développement institutionnel des sciences religieuses en France", *Archives de sociologie des religions*, No. 21, January–June 1966, pp. 23–6.

is not an object of historical study, even though the historians (witness the work of Gabriel Le Bras) did not wait for Vatican II in order to take account of the problem within their own sphere. The "history of salvation" does not originate with or depend on the historical disciplines, which know only *a* history of salvation connected with Judaeo-Christian tradition, and therefore comparable with other such histories for the purpose of determining its degree of originality. And of course the "ecumenical movement" is a term which runs the risk of referring to a quite different content depending on whether the individual using it is an historian or a theologian. And then there is the point that a rigorous study of "modernism" or of "integrism" can be carried out without having to be subject to the obsolete interventions of the magisterium or the subsequent development of theology.

One has to be specially vigilant with regard to another kind of slip. On the pretext that Christianity is an *historical* religion, nothing often seems more normal or legitimate than a perpetual to-and-fro between an historical understanding of the Church and an ecclesial understanding of history. That each may be of interest to the other is indisputable, but it does not follow that they enjoy the same epistemological status and partake of the same intellectual procedure. The historian does not restrict his inquiry to what was objectively the Church's work: he extends it to the whole interplay of observable images: the one that the Church had of itself at a given moment, the one that it gave of itself for the benefit of various groups, the image that it had of these various groups. Without such an analysis, it is impossible, for example, to understand anything of the *Syllabus of Errors* and the condemnation of "liberalism". In addition, any conflict within the Church, such as was to be observed in regard to the *Syllabus* among liberal and Ultramontane Catholics, shows that several series of images can coexist and conflict within the bosom of the Church.

When the theologian speaks of the Church's self-understanding, the historian records a plurality of understandings, of which one—that which is dominant—tends to impose itself as the only valid one. If he is of a pessimistic temperament, history will seem to him in this respect to be a long sequence of monopolies, oppositions and reversals, in which each new stage or aspect undertakes retroactively to correct the past: the present manufactures history according to its needs. Hence he will see "social Catholicism", born of the intransigent Catholicism of the *Syllabus*, rediscovering a filiation with what it calls "integrism"— which is none other than its fraternal enemy "integral Catholicism". Above all, what has occurred before our eyes during the last ten or twenty years should teach us a lesson: out of all the dominant "histories", none has been able to resist the onslaught of new situations, which have precipitately forced us into a revision of all that we had previously learned. This is an interesting experience for the historian, who is forced to see that his usual parameters depend on his position, and that his position can be affected at any moment. But over and above all these fluctuations, the safest way, and the only one to take, is the way of a systematic consideration of the conditions governing the elaboration of any historical product.

As time passes, the past grows blurred and easily enters the realm of the imaginary. A society cannot live without a past; it *commemorates* this past in various ways, whereas the historian's concern is to try to *"remember"* it as it was. Hence the sometimes considerable divergences between the two methods of representing the past. Certain periods are privileged and idealized. Until quite recently the understanding of the Church just passed the Middle Ages by. When historical research made any romantic representation of the period impossible, what happened was a kind of juxtapositioning of *two* Middle Ages: that of the historians, and the other (which was a system, and a model in the two senses of the word)—the Christian society, which could be opposed to the dominant model of "modern society".

The primitive Church also played (and continues to play) this part of a model, independently of the research work carried out into Christian origins. But in this area, in addition to the dissociation effect noted above, there is a blockage effect. Confronted with the image of its origins offered to it by history, the Church began by refusing to recognize itself. The image did not merely seem disagreeable or distorted, but ruinous as far as its foundations were concerned. The only possible explanation in its eyes was that, whatever their disposition, the historians were merely affording proof of *their* lack of understanding. In fact, it might well be (thus the argument would run) that the historian was biased, his thesis was insufficiently stratified, or his conclusions too adventurous; in return, their critique might be well established and the threat a real one; but of course this sort of rejection did not suffice to ward off the new evidence: the reconsiderations, which were often deep-reaching, prevailed—as the modernist crisis, seen in its entirety, shows. What is important in this regard is not so much the details of this or that plaint, valid or not, but the sense of a collective effort pursued through an entire century, and the way which is being taken today. No judgment passed on any particular historian has any meaning except when this overall balance of the account is taken into consideration. Two important phenomena are to be observed: on the one hand, once the shock has passed, better relations are established between rival disciplines; on the other hand, this patient reconquest of a distant past becomes significant in the present as the motor of a rational evolution induced by religious ideas and images. Hence the appearance of a new and major fact for consideration: the intervention—in the play of the religious *consciousness*—of the religious *sciences*, the increments of which, relayed from circuit to circuit, eventually descend to the body of the faithful.

But talk of misunderstanding also brings in a theme which is still implicit or obscured: one can understand *only from within*. Only the Christian, he who possesses the faith, can truly understand Christianity; the unbeliever cannot do so. This thesis has never been systematically developed. It works on two levels: one theological, the other psychological. In fact, those who employ the argument refer more often to a consensus psychology than to a thesis regarding the act of faith. And knowledge from "within" is not the privileged possession of religious groups alone; it is one of the laws of social life. For the historian, however, it is neither a necessary nor a sufficient condition for his vocation. Things are very much more complex than that.

Certainly the historian's *familiarity* with his field is indispensable for him: it is a fundamental aspect of his competence. But group membership is perhaps neither the sole nor the best way of acquiring it. In addition, it is only one of the aspects of historical work, which implies a constant dialectic of subjectivity and objectivity and, in order to ensure this, an epistemological break with mere, simple acquaintance with the commonly held view. But, even at this level, familiarity is only one aspect of reality, precisely because of the partitioning effect that it has. If *only the believer* can talk about the faith, it must also be true that *only the unbeliever* can talk about *atheism*. To judge by results, indeed, this would never seem to be taken into account: it is mostly the believers who write about atheism, and Catholic intellectuals about the dechristianization of the proletariat.

Psychology has shown quite clearly to what extent self-consciousness can be false consciousness, the product of illusions and compensation, but also how there is no consciousness other than social consciousness—group-integrated consciousness, not in an isolated ghetto, but within a communications process which does not abolish boundaries but relativizes them. The image that I offer of myself can be more significent in regard to my own understanding than my self-image. Any total knowledge of a phenomena requires several different approaches, and is both interpersonal and interdisciplinary. The case of ethnology is enlightening here: what is it, in fact, if not knowledge from without and from above? But this is not an everlasting situation. One day we shall be seeing African or Asiatic ethnologists come to examine our European societies, just as some North-American ethnologists already so. The new view is indispensable.

There is still another direction to explore. The separation between believers and unbelievers is not absolute, not only in the sense that each has its degrees, but because there are crossings over from one to the other. There is the believer who has "lost the faith" and the unbeliever who has been "converted"; the priest who has been laicized and the widower who takes orders, and so on. In our pluralistic society, the opportunities of dual participation are not lacking: one has only to think of the young Christian who has been educated only in state schools—from the first grade to the university, that is, the Christian whose faith has developed in a sociologically composite, and both institutionally and ideologically secular, milieu. And then there are the young people who have always been wholly without religious affiliation, but whose families have sent them to a Catholic college where there is a daily eucharist and a director of consciences.

Eventually, the principle of knowledge "from within" would lead to a veritable paralysis of scientific activity by an increasingly extreme partitioning. Only the Frenchman would be able to talk about France, the peasant about the countryside, the Catholic about the Roman division of the Church, and the Jesuits about the Society of Jesus. This is no illusory image: how many times has one heard the argument that the Roman congregations were incapable of understanding French, German or American Catholicism, or that the clergy were essentially incompetent in matters of marriage and economics? These are difficulties of intercomprehension, which the historian encounters all the time and which is not the least fascinating of all the problems proper to his vocation. To go further, there is the example of the Abbé Bremond, who regretted that he was not himself a mystic, in order better to understand the mystics with whom he was concerned. And there is the question of how a man of our times can be sure that he can understand the centuries of the past, and enter into the profound emotions of men who can no longer speak out today, and perhaps never wrote a line. There is no longer any means of access from within, unless one is to define human nature apart from all reference to historicity.

I shall conclude these various observations by listing the ideas by which they are oriented—which perhaps have only the value that attaches to a personal viewpoint.

1. The pure historian dreams of a universal history which allows each phenomenon its objective place. But in a society where man has always been inimical to man, and where the "truce of God" was only an ephemeral institution in a community torn by conflicts and confrontations, where Christianity is far from appearing a factor of peace and unity, he knows that he is always writing a partisan form of history and that its dominant form is always the history of the dominant party, of the victor of the moment. He knows, too, that in the human condition the "pure" historian is only a dream. The objective techniques that he develops are directed not only to the critical analysis of his documents but to the always incomplete mastery of his own individual and social subjectivity. More than one imagines, history is a form of *ascesis*, less by virtue of the lessons that it offers than

of its exigences. The historian who lives his subject is primarily a man involved in a struggle with himself.

2. The first task of history—and that of Church history in particular—is to exist: to know how it should be constituted and how it is to understand itself. That is not so simple as it may appear. In spite of the work done, there are still vast unexplored prospects, even if one considers only modern and contemporary history; and the work done is often far from answering our questions and according with our norms. In these conditions, *to exist* means to prevail, to take up one's rights and defend one's liberty. History does not cease having to confront a general conception of the past, connected with the global image that each church offers itself in regard to its mission and its development: the study of confessional text-books (and, from the opposite view, of secular text-books) is full of relevant examples. Consequently, there are the cases of resistance that mean that all of any one history is not acceptable at any particular moment, that certain cruces will at first be rejected by a religious group without any critical examination (for instance, the difficulties that Albert Houtin, the historian of modernism, experienced with his bishop for having denied the historicity of Saint Réné, the first bishop of Angers, who was recently scrubbed off the Church's calendar); and that even a specific critical analysis can merely serve to reveal the constraining power of certain ideas (for instance, all the discussions, under Pius X, in favour of the historical actuality of the│flying holy house of Loretto); or of certain currents of thought (for example, the anti-liberalism up to 1914 and beyond, and, in the same way, the reaction to it once the means of expression were available).

3. The historian cannot really escape the profusion of self-images which appear in the Church, whether successively or simultaneously. On the one hand, they are on different levels, each with its own epistemological status; their very diversity giving rise to opposition, and an incomplete understanding of the actual identity of certain standpoints producing confusion. On the other hand, they refer to multiple currents of thought, each one inspiring its own historiography. The historian's task is to bring order into this confusion, to make paths through the forest, to obtain a perspective if possible, and—in this Babel of

tongues—to be the intermediary, the interpreter between people who sometimes are more sharply aware of what separates them than of what unites them, and—more often than not—do not even succeed in clarifying their arguments. But at the same time, everything in his discipline—documents, techniques, colleagues— forces him to break with the confessional restriction of these arguments, to refuse the language of his sources in order to develop his own language in dependence on his methodological requirements. At the same time as he works for his Church, the Catholic historian has inevitably to follow his own and proper path without allowing himself to be stopped by any particular frontier.

4. The historian is aware to what extent his discipline is uncertain of itself, for all the above-mentioned reasons, how it advances with difficulty, and that it is not always clear how it progresses. But he also knows that the way taken is irreversible. The history of history, for a century and a half, leaves no room for doubt on this point. Even disagreements between different schools cannot prevail against the reality which constitutes the community of historians today. All historians today—whether in the history of religion or not—practise a radically secularized approach which can call upon various types of understanding. This is a problem to which no one as yet has given enough impartial attention. Nevertheless it is possible to reject hasty classifications attached to inexplicit options, which might, for example, reject the Marxist "explanation" while allowing a privileged position to an "ecumenical" understanding as more authentically religious. The historical method cannot function appropriately on this ideological level. A close analysis would soon show, on the contrary, that each type of understanding, even if it has its limitations and manifest inadequacies of comprehension, also has its own truth and lucidity: the historian can describe the curves of influence of the liberal Catholicism and Ultramontane Catholicism of the last century, but he cannot allow one to be right and the other wrong. Such Manichaeism would have to suppose that one of the two, and only that one, had a right understanding of "modern society". It is sufficient to know the documentary history of both to be aware that such a judgment is far from the truth: liberalism was open to values ignored by the intransigent approach, yet the latter marked

out deficiencies to which the first was insensitive; and both of them were incapable of grasping the points which made socialism so successful.

5. To postulate the specificity of historical studies implies their discontinuity with reflective theology. Each can go so far as to take the other as its object, but historical theology and the history of Christian thought will always remain two distinct areas. The historical understanding of the Church cannot be of the same order as the ecclesial or theological understanding of history. Of course, for the Church, history (as it constitutes itself) is the location of its self-understanding: but does this formulation which has so imposed itself on our culture represent progress in the course of coming to understand its mystery, or is it no more than a mode of speaking in the language of our own times? And can the historian remain satisfied with this indetermination (the reasons for which are not clear to him) between the Church of the fullness of divine life and the historical Church at a given moment in its development within a complex interaction of oppositions: to what it was at another time, to what it is capable of becoming, to the internal divisions which it undergoes, to other historical formations—churches, sects and various currents—which derive from the same founder and from the same tradition?

It is not at all necessary to be an exegete to see that the Church began in incomprehension. The disciples could not hear what Christ said to them: it was too much for them; they had to wait for the coming of the Spirit. After Pentecost, their horizons were arrested first of all at the notion of the Jewish community; the intervention of Paul was necessary in order to change that. Then there was the question of the imminence of the Parousia. And so one could go on: history, in this view, has never stopped. Will that be the countenance of the Church for all time to come? Perhaps it is only a law of its development, as of all human societies. But it is true that this particular collection of phenomena, whose continuity is so impressive, has been effectively taken into account by Christian historiography, but less by reflective theology. Every great historical expression—Communism as well as capitalism—has its dark side: what seems to be the language of the believer himself, of the supporter, is for the outsider a trustworthy expression of the very essence of the phenomenon itself.

It can be seen why, beyond that point which is common to their disciplines, and therefore where they can partially coincide, history and theology are not identical. More than for any individual subject, the lack of approximation is constant and irreducible, between the self-consciousness of a group on the one hand—its identity—and its expressive forms on the other. The theologian starts with the *identity*, and the historian with the written, institutional, lived and other *expressions*. The second can grasp the consciousness which is mediated by all these extremely diverse manifestations, but he has not, by himself, any means of grasping the identity to which they bear witness. And the theologian can never deduce the consciousness of the Church from what he knows of its identity: it is in seeing it deploy itself in time that he seizes in practice the mystery of this identity.

Historians and theologians are intermediaries and interpreters. Do the theologians really think that they are on sure ground in talking of the Church's self-understanding? In the eyes of the historians, such an understanding can never be more than a symbolic expression of a hope: they see the reality as consisting of a plurality of localized self-understandings. The best that they can aspire to do is to understand themselves as agents of intercomprehension.

However, the historian can never resign himself to this plurality as if it were the last word on his research and his responsibilities. There is an immense amount of comparative work, terribly neglected until now, waiting for him in conjunction with the representatives of the other social sciences, in order to construct appropriate models, develop a typology, and in this way to pass beyond the banal implications of the old formula of a Christianity one and undivided.

Translated by John Griffiths

Norbert Brox

Forms of Christianity in the Primitive Church

I. INTRODUCTION

IT IS very difficult to provide an objective and systematic outline of the different types of Christianity that existed in the earliest years of the Church. Thanks, however, to the advanced stage of historical research, we now know enough to be able to say that, as far as the factual differences between theological thinking in the primitive Church are concerned, the first Palestinian communities were not the same as the Hellenistic communities founded by, at the time of, or before, Paul. Different types of Church community began to emerge at a very early stage indeed, but this phenomenon becomes really interesting only when we try to judge whether—and when—the Church began to see itself in an "essentially" changed light.

This is difficult to do on the basis of purely historical criteria, and many questions are raised. To what extent does, for example, a different terminology imply a change in the Church's understanding of itself? Or does this denote the same understanding expressed in a different language? Where do we reach the point when we can no longer speak about the same understanding? Should we look for differences in the Church's doctrine or rather in the changing patterns of thinking and expressing ideas at the time? Or, so long as it is simply a question of the orthodox forms of the Church, is it enough to retain Augustine's distinctions, accepted throughout the patristic and medieval periods, *non iam adversi, etsi diversi* (En. in Ps. 47, 3; PL, 36, 534)?[1] None of these questions has been satisfactorily answered by Church historians using modern hermeneutical methods.[2]

In this case, the problem is made more difficult by the sources. The main sources for the first Palestinian community are Gal. 1. 2 (little information), the Acts of the Apostles and the synoptic gospels. The Acts, however, tell us less about the historical Jesus than the synoptics. They were, after all, written at the end of the first century under the influence of Greek-speaking Christians who were not seeking to record the events that had taken place in the early Church. The historical material dealing with the early Palestinian communities also seems to have been very slender. The synoptics, on the other hand, are valuable sources mainly because of traditional conclusions,[3] in particular with regard to the *logia* ("Q"; see below).

In other words, we have only a few indirect, fragmentary and uncertain pieces of evidence and very much is still unknown. Above all, we have no authentic verbal tradition of the Jerusalem apostles and very few short, though important, liturgical texts (e.g., Rom. 1. 3 f.; 1 Cor. 11. 23–25; 15. 3–5). The way in which the Pauline communities understood themselves can be reconstructed from the letters of Paul, and the same applies to the Hellenistic communities which came about independently of Paul. If the "basis" of the communal theology is used rather

---

[1] See H. de Lubac, "À propos de la formule: 'Diversi, sed non adversi' ", in *Recherches de science religieuse* 40 (1951–1952), pp. 27–40.

[2] See H. Köser, "ΓΝΩΜΑΙ ΔΙΑΦΟΡΟΙ. Ursprung und Wesen der Mannigfaltigkeit in der Geschichte des frühen Christentums", in *Zeitschrift für Theologie und Kirche* 65 (1968), pp. 160–203; English: *Harvard Theological Review* 58 (1965), pp. 279–318. Köster's answer, which would have been easier to verify by assessing historical documents in the concrete than by Köster's analytical process, is: "It is a question as to whether the historical event of the terrestrial Jesus of Nazareth is effective as a criterion of the proclamation of the Christian message and of Christian theology, not necessarily as the content of that theology" (p. 163); in other words, it is a question of "going back again and again to the origin of Christian faith, to Jesus" (p. 203).

[3] See H. J. Cadbury's critical comments in "Gospel Study and Our Image of Early Christianity", in *Journal of Bibl. Lit.* 83 (1964), pp. 139–145.

than the theology of Paul and his leading opponents, then the historical approach is only a tentative quest.

It is important to list these difficulties because they show that my attempt to outline the different forms of very early Christianity is of necessity based, not on an examination of complete models, but only on the analysis of a few elements. In the following section (II), I shall briefly set out these elements of the early Church's self-understanding and, in the final section (III), compare and contrast them with each other.

II. HISTORICAL SURVEY

1. The Primitive Jewish Christian Community

This first Church cannot be confined to Jerusalem, because the risen Jesus also "appeared" in Galilee (see Mark 14. 28; 16. 7; Matt. 28. 16–20; John 21).[4] We know nothing about these Galilean or Palestinian communities except that they existed, but we do have a little information about the community in Jerusalem. Its members did not depart from Jewish religious practice (see Acts 2. 46; 3. 1; 5. 12, 42; 10. 14), but separated themselves from Judaism by calling themelves "saints", the "elect" or the "community of God", by practising a special baptismal rite of initiation and by celebrating together the presence of Jesus in a meal in their homes—not in the temple.[5] As the new people of God, their eschatological community or ἐκκλησία was visibly separated, then, from the older qāhāl and they soon made their missionary intention known. The twelve retained their functions as witnesses of the Easter event (1 Cor. 15. 5) and as representatives of the new Israel,[6] with the eschatological task of judging the Israel of their own time (Matt. 19. 28).

---

[4] G. Schille has opposed with almost exaggerated emphasis the idea that Jerusalem enjoyed a monopoly as the original Christian cell, using textual analysis as a weapon against the traditional reliance of Church historians on the Acts of the Apostles; see his *Anfänge der Kirche. Erwägungen zur apostolischen Frühgeschichte* (Munich, 1966).

[5] A. Vögtle, for example, provides a number of details in his excellent contribution on the primitive community ("Die Urgemeinde"), in R. Kottje and B. Moeller, *Ökumenische Kirchengeschichte*, I (Mainz and Munich, 1970), pp. 25–36.

[6] The function and the pre-eminent place of the twelve do not seem to have been important for very long. In contrast to Acts 1. 15 ff., according to which Matthias was elected to replace Judas and to make up the

Because they were loyal to the Jewish law, they were tolerated, but they were also endangered by their proclamation to
the whole of the Jewish people of the message of salvation
through faith in the resurrection (Rom. 1. 3 ff.). As far as we
know, their first open conflict with the Jews resulted in the
execution of James the son of Zebedee (ca. A.D. 44).

This community soon ceased to be the only representative of
Christianity, but, because we know nothing concrete about the
other communities, we cannot assume that they differed radically from the community in Jerusalem, which was, however,
undoubtedly very pluriform both theologically and structurally.
We can, for example, discern a clear formation of opposing
groups there in the controversy over the conditions of the
mission to the gentiles, and even more in the so-called Council
of Jerusalem. On the one hand, there were the Judaizers who
opposed Paul (see Gal. 2. 4) and, on the other, the pro-Pauline
group under Peter and James, who must himself have exerted a
Judaizing influence, especially in ritual matters (see Gal. 2. 12).

There was a great difference in attitude towards the mission
outside Palestine between these two groups, and even more between them and the third group of Greek-speaking Hellenists or
proselytes who had come to Jerusalem from the diaspora, had
been converted at a very early stage and, because of various tensions, had formed themselves into a group in opposition to the
Aramaic-speaking Jews. Their leaders were the "seven" so-called
"deacons" who cared for the poor and widows (see Acts 6) and
who were, to judge from their names (Stephen, Philip and
Nicolaus), Greek. These Hellenists from the diaspora inevitably
adhered less strictly to the law and cultic practices, and their
preaching was full of Jesus' more explosive, critical teachings.
This led to serious conflict with the Jewish authorities. Stephen,
for example, was accused of saying "that this Jesus of Nazareth
will destroy this place and will change the customs which Moses
delivered to us" (Acts 6. 14; see also 6. 11–13; 7. 48, 53), an ac-
cusation which was, of course, connected with the charge levelled

---

symbolic number of apostles, when James the son of Zebedee died in
about A.D. 44, there was no thought of electing a replacement, and as
such the twelve did not have any authoritative function at the Council
of Jerusalem of A.D. 48–49.

against Jesus for threatening to "destroy the temple" (Mark 14. 58). Persecuted and banished, many of the Hellenists continued to preach outside Jerusalem and Palestine—in Samaria and Syria. This marked the beginning of the long non-Jewish, Hellenistic and very diverse development of Christianity. Yet it is most important to recognize the diversity of Christian "self-understanding" that existed in the very earliest Palestinian community,[7] a diversity which became crystallized in the attitude towards Judaism. The questions which inevitably arise, but which can be answered better when we come to consider the primitive gentile community (see II, 2 below), are, for example, can we really speak here of different conceptions of the early Church? Is it possible to refer to a qualitatively different way of approaching Jesus? Now, however, we must complete our brief survey of the early Jewish community.

Historical research into the synoptic tradition has resulted in the isolation of a definite group of very early Jewish Christians whose testimony can be reconstructed as the *logia* (Q) in Matthew and Luke.[8] These Jewish Christians had a sense of mission (Luke 10. 2–16, 21 ff.) as followers of Jesus (Matt. 8. 21 ff.; Luke 14. 27), the Son of Man (Luke 9. 57 ff.). An urgent theme was the conflict in which they were involved with "this generation", and which arose because of their proclamation of the coming of the Son of Man and of his words, which they heard, explained and collected with great care. Acting on his words was above all important to them (Luke 6. 46–49), and this too resulted in conflict, because it required love of one's enemies and mercy, not hatred and hostility. All this was, moreover, closely related to the Jewish political resistance to the Roman occupation. Under

[7] O. Cullmann is very informative in this connection in his article "La diversité des types de Christianisme dans l'Eglise primitive", in *Studi e Materiali di Storia delle Religioni* 38 (1967), pp. 175–84. Cullmann does not present the early hstory of the Church simply as a diversity between groups, but rather as a lack of unity because the Jewish Christians refused to support Stephen and his companions (Acts 8. 1), Peter and James the son of Zebedee (Acts 12. 2, 17), and finally Paul—especially when he was imprisoned in Jerusalem (Acts 21).

[8] For the sake of brevity, I would mention only P. Hoffmann, "Die Anfänge der Theologie in der Logienquelle", in J. Schreiner, ed., *Gestalt und Anspruch des Neuen Testamentes* (Würzburg, 1969), pp. 134–52, who also lists the most important books and articles.

the banner of Jesus, these Jews opposed armed conflict and actively supported peace, but their attempt failed and the Roman-Jewish War took place (ca. A.D. 66–70).

Their interpretation of Jesus' message was of course very much conditioned by the prevailing historical and political circumstances, but what is striking is that it had nothing to do with the Mosaic law. One particularly interesting aspect of this early Jewish Christian community (which had a "model of Christian self-understanding": namely, a specifically political one, which was "different from that of other groups, though it confessed the same faith"[9]) is that this group made a very individual—and for us unacceptable—selection in its interpretation of Jesus' life and message by excluding such essential elements as his suffering and resurrection. We may therefore conclude that the differences between these various "models of Christian self-understanding" are almost always the result of differences in selection and emphasis, and it is this that gives rise to the basic question of continuity and "norm" in all interpretations.

2. The Early Gentile Christian Community

The epistles provide us with more, though by no means all theological and historical details about this community. Banished from Jerusalem, the Jewish Hellenists had begun missionary work among the gentiles in mixed gentile and Jewish territories successfully long before Paul, who joined these communities after his conversion. For a long time, the centre of this new "mixed" Christianity was Antioch, where a new phase in the history of the Gospel was enacted—it was proclaimed not only in a new place, but also in a new way.

Very briefly, what happened was that either the terminology of the Jewish Christians ("Son of Man", "servant of God", "Messiah", etc.) ceased to be used because it was not understood by gentiles who stood outside the Old Testament tradition, or else it was reinterpreted in accordance with the gentiles' Hellenistic way of thinking. (Examples of this are "Son of God" and "Lord".)[10] What we have to consider here are certain aspects of

---

[9] See P. Hoffmann, op. cit., p. 151.
[10] See, for example, W. G. Kümmel, Die Theologie des Neuen Testa-

the Jewish law as a criterion for the interpretation of the Christian message as opposed to the history of its origins, and the question of the part played by the Jesus tradition in the idea that these gentile communities had of themselves.

In the first place, we must remember that, although the Jewish law was not in itself a problem to the gentile Christians, the Jewish Christians *made* it into a problem for them. They had been converted by Hellenists—Christians who did not observe the Jewish law or practise circumcision—and, unlike the Jewish Christians of Palestine, did not unquestioningly accept these practices as necessary to salvation. This situation in the mixed communities of Jews and gentiles in Antioch and elsewhere, however, led after a few years of freedom from the law to conflicts, because a coexistence that was subject to the Jewish ritual conditions which were eventually imposed was found to be impossible. This was not, however, primarily the problem of the Hellenistic Jewish Christians there (or of the gentile Christians), but of the Palestinian Christians who, seeing that their image of Christianity was being called into question, demanded that the gentiles should be separated and at the same time circumcised as a condition of baptism.

Before the emergence of these urgent problems, however, the Hellenistic Church was untroubled by the Jewish law and the practice of circumcision, that is, by the question of the historical origin of the Christian faith and its connection with the Judaism of Jesus himself. In other words, these early gentile Christians had simply not considered the necessity of unity with the Jewish Christian Church. This is, of course, astonishing because it presents us with a form of Christianity which had moved away, after only a few years, from the original soil of the Jesus tradition into a very different environment.

It was mainly Paul who was responsible for bringing this period of separation from Judaism to a close. The relationship between the Jewish law (and circumcision) and Christian faith was a problem that had been introduced into Paul's purely gentile communities from outside, both by agitation on the part of

ments nach seinen Hauptzeugen Jesus, Paulus, Johannes (Göttingen, 1969), pp. 93-111.

the Judaizers and by intercommunication between the individual communities. What is more, in his sermons, Paul, the erstwhile zealous Jew, continued to argue against the law and for faith, and to interpret lack of faith as disobedience and hardness of heart.

We should not, however, imagine that this was the only type of preaching known in the Hellenistic communities. The letters of Paul and the first stages of the way of the Gospel were both very much concerned with it. But neither of these came within the experience of the gentiles who had been converted to Christianity and who, as is clear from the writings of Paul, had a very different way of looking at faith. Because of the very different climate of thought in which they lived, their attitude towards faith was inevitably different. For example, they placed a different emphasis on worship, the sacraments and the idea of the Spirit, and they understood man dualistically and Christ soteriologically (in striking contrast to the traditional Jewish-Christian view of Christ).

It is hardly possible to ascertain whether these early gentile Christian communities were introduced to the Jewish Old Testament tradition, in which Christianity had originated and with which they had no living connection, by the Hellenistic Jewish missionaries, or whether those missionaries sought to establish a permanent historical link between the Old Testament tradition and Christianity by means of scriptural evidence (using, of course, the Septuagint). This is a problem which we shall have to examine below.

In the meantime, however, we must bear in mind in this context that these Hellenistic Christians had no knowledge of the "Jesus tradition", that is, of Jesus' words and actions. The mainstays of Paul's theology were, it should be remembered, not so much the few elements of the tradition of Jesus' words which he recorded in his letters (he makes no mention at all, for example, of Jesus' miracles), but above all the basic events of Jesus' death and resurrection. We are, I think, bound to assume that continuity with the Jesus tradition of the early Palestinian Jewish communities was on a much narrower basis in Paul's churches. Finally, therefore, we are led to ask whether these differences between the primitive Jewish and the early Hellenistic Christian communities in understanding the origin of Jesus are relevant or irrelevant.

A very important factor revealed by the sources is that there were many different forms of Christianity in the early gentile Church as well. Once again, however, it is not possible to find very much reliable information about these groups, or, for example, to identify with any certainty the few which Paul called opponents and heretics. There is a general tendency at present to speak of gnostic "models of Christian self-understanding", on the one hand predominantly Hellenistic and, on the other, Judaizing. Most of the recently attempted reconstructions are, however, too unsound in their method for us to place any reliance on their conclusions that the early gentile communities were of a gnostic type.[11]

Although they are by no means complete, a number of data can, however, be listed. In the first place, the very difficulties experienced by the local gentile Christian communities, and Paul's polemics, point to the existence of different groups with very divergent views. One clear indication of this divergence is the considerable mutual disagreement between various groups and between them and Paul (see 1 Cor. 8 and 10; Rom. 4) about the interpretation and the concrete Christian understanding of taboos, knowledge, love, and above all freedom.

The conflict among the Christians at Corinth is another sign of this diversity of opinion. The conflict arose because one powerful group taught that pneumatic and charismatic phenomena were the pre-eminent criteria for Christian faith (see 1 Cor. 12–14). This contention was disputed by Paul, who insisted that faith had above all to be communicated and used to build up the community of believers. In this type of Christianity, an extreme enthusiasm for manifestations of the Spirit seems to have gone together with a Christology concentrated almost exclusively on

---

[11] The most representative theses have been analysed, for example, by R. Haardt, in "Gnosis und Neues Testament", in *Bibel und zeitgemässer Glaube, ed. J. Sint* (Klosterneuburg, Vienna and Munich, 1967), pp. 131–158; *ibid.*, "Gnosis", in *Sacramentum Mundi*, II (London and New York, 1968), pp. 476–86; W. C. van Unnik, "Die Gedanken der Gnostiker über die Kirche", in *Vom Christus zur Kirche*, ed. J. Giblet (Vienna, 1966), pp. 223–38, especially p. 225.

the risen Lord, the *Kyrios*, and ignoring the crucified Jesus (see 1 Cor. 12. 3; 1. 18 ff.; 2. 2).

There were also those remarkable groups which apparently came about as the result of an erroneous interpretation of the authentic meaning of baptism—only some of these confessed adherence to Christ (see 1 Cor. 1. 12 ff.). This may also have been connected with the specifically Hellenistic interpretation of the sacraments—Paul himself was also influenced by these "magical" ideas (1 Cor. 11. 29 f.; 15. 29). We may therefore conclude that the Church at Corinth had a very complex and pluriform structure and that it was from this complexity that the question of the criterion and the norm of the Christian faith arose.

Yet another version of Christianity emerges from Paul's second letter to the Corinthians, this time in the form of a renewed Judaization, which was, however, very different to that attempted in the Christian communities in Galatia. It would, of course, be wrong to identify every attempt to restore the Jewish law and its *theologoumena* with orthodox Jewish nomism. What happened in most cases was that mythical elements were combined with a return to the Old Testament tradition, with heterodox results.

Further indications of diversity in Christianity can be found in the fragment of the letter in Phil. 3, the far-reaching cosmic orientation of the teaching in the letters to the Colossians and the Ephesians and the very different conception of the expectation of an imminent second coming in 1 Thessalonians, which can hardly be reconciled with faith in the resurrection. The opponents to whom Paul refers in his letter to the Galatians were certainly not gentile Christians, or a gnostic or "gnosticizing" group, but orthodox Jews who were hostile to Paul and wanted to impose the law and circumcision on their gentile fellow Christians. According to Luke, the tradition of Apollos (Acts 14. 24–19. 6) seems to have been a special version of the proclamation of the Christian message which was recognized (1 Cor. 3. 6), but was in some way incomplete (Acts 18. 26; 19. 4 f.). As a final example let me mention only the different tradition of Philip (Acts 8. 5 ff.; 21. 8 f.).[12]

[12] A. Ehrhardt has discussed this in detail in "Christianity before the

This pluriformity in the understanding of the Christian message clearly marked the beginning of a problem which arose again and again throughout the later history of the Church, the problem of choice between the popular faith of the Christian community and the more deeply reflected, theological understanding of one or more groups. Within the context of our subject, however, this is only a special version of the whole phenomenon.

III. VARIATIONS AND DIFFERENCES

Very marked differences can be perceived in the various ways in which the Church was understood by the first Christians. These differences are revealed, or have to be inferred from the diversity of models of the early Christian communities. The modern historian regards the continuity, identity and unity of the early Church with its great diversity of forms as a problem, but the first Christians were not conscious of this. One has the impression that the primitive gentile community interpreted the resurrection cultically, sacramentally and soteriologically in many different ways, but lived in close union with the risen Christ without knowing or needing to know very much about the Jewish Christian teaching of the Jesus tradition.

In the early Jewish Church in Palestine, on the other hand, faith in Jesus was made explicit in indigenous categories, and by stressing the history of Jesus and the foundation of his community. These Jewish Christians were above all concerned, in their faith in Jesus, with the salvation of Israel and, at the end of time, that of the gentiles as well (Matt. 8. 11).

The Palestinian origins of the kerygma was, however, not relevant in the same way to the gentile converts. This is borne out by their early freedom from the law. Their position cannot really be compared with that of Paul, who could only think of faith and the Church in contrast to and in continuity with Judaism. It is not likely that scriptural evidence had the same meaning for his communities of non-Jewish converts as it had for Paul himself.

Apostles' Creed", in the *Harvard Theological Review* 55 (1962), pp. 73–119, especially pp. 80–92.

The very fact that collections were made for the Church in Jerusalem (Gal. 2. 10; 1 Cor. 16; 2 Cor. 8. f.; Rom. 15. 25-27) shows how convinced Paul was that it was necessary to remain permanently linked to the first Jewish community (he called it "my service", ἡ διακονία μου, Rom. 15. 31), because it was theologically impossible for him to deny the Jewish origin of Jesus. Would, however, Macedonia and Achaia have been eager to contribute towards the Church in Jerusalem in the light of their own understanding of the Church and without having been urged by Paul (Rom. 15. 26 f.)?[13]

The gentile Christians were certainly informed about the continuity of Israel with the historical Jesus, but this tradition certainly does not seem to have been the basis of their faith as it was for Paul, who interpreted the mission to the gentiles in the light of the ultimate conversion of Israel (see Rom. 9-11). In other words, it was not at all easy for the gentiles to understand and adhere to Paul's image of the Church based on the history of Israel, or to his emphasis on the historical Jesus as the most important criterion for faith (see 1 Cor.). The inevitable consequence of this is that his gentile communities did not hand down his understanding of the Church, but a very different one.

Yet, despite Paul's insistence on the Jewish origin of the gentile Church (Rom. 11. 11-24), what is remarkable is that Palestinian Christianity gave way with so little sign of crisis to the gentile Church, virtually disappearing in the Jewish war.[14] The earliest post-Easter preaching about salvation in Jesus was very closely related to personal traditions (Peter, James, the twelve), and geographical traditions (Galilee, Jerusalem). A Christology of the resurrection without homological Easter stories was unthinkable at that time and in that place, and, according to Paul, was, in its Palestinian version, part of the original tradition of faith in the qualified sense (see 1 Cor. 15. 2 ff.). Yet, to judge from all that

---

[13] One aspect of this problem is, of course, the need for a sign of unity with the Church in Jerusalem on the part of the gentile Christians—the collection would fulfil this need. The other side of the question, however, is Paul's fear that the "saints" in Jerusalem might not accept the collection—they might, in other words, reject Church unity with the gentiles (Rom. 15. 31).

[14] From the point of view of the Church as a whole, Jerusalem and its bishop became important again in the fourth century, after Constantine.

can be learnt from the fragments of pre-Pauline confessions of faith and hymns (see, for example, Phil. 2. 6 ff.; 1 Tim. 3. 16) of the gentile teaching about Christ, this had, in a surprisingly short time, become very different indeed. In this teaching, events "concerning Jesus of Nazareth" (Luke 24. 19) were described which extended from the other world into this world and the coming of the divine redeemer was emphasized.

The Jewish Church stood directly in the tradition of the Easter witnesses, whose testimony stressed this continuity with Jesus. The early gentile Christians, on the other hand, did not base their faith on this tradition. They grasped the fact that the kerygma was closely related to the name of Jesus, but it was developed in very different, specifically Hellenistic ideas about the redemption.

Another significant fact is that it was in a Hellenistic environment—in Antioch—that the community of believers, which had received a distinctively Palestinian theology, was first recognized as an independent group and given the special name of "Christians" (Acts 11. 26). Further historical proof is provided by the fact that, immediately preceding this, the Jews in Jerusalem had been persecuting and banishing, not all the followers of Jesus, but only the Hellenists.

We may therefore conclude that the first Christians differed very widely and at a very early stage and above all not simply about the question of the Jewish law. They understood their historical links with the origins of the Church in very different ways and they developed very different Christologies.

These differences can to some extent be perceived in the danger to which the Christian community in Jerusalem was from the very beginning exposed—a reversion to the law, the temple and pre-Christian rigidity. This, of course, did not happen in the case of the gentile Christians, who were challenged by other ideologies and practices.

The differences cannot be reduced to simple orthodoxy and heresy; the crucial point was Paul's teaching which stressed above all the identity of the crucified and the exalted Jesus (1 Cor. 1. 23; 12. 3). The distance between the various early Christian communities can most easily be measured by this criterion,[15] which

[15] In *Religion in Geschichte und Gegenwart* VI (1962), p. 1190, W. G. Kümmel said: "This (Paul's) historical proclamation of salvation gave

soon became a conscious "norm" for faith—that every interpretation of Christianity in all its diversity has to be judged by what is said about the history of Jesus.

In its Jesus tradition and Easter witness, the early Jewish community clearly related faith to the history of Jesus and this model was inevitably changed by the mission to the gentiles. What is so evident in the theology of Paul, the Jewish apostle to the gentiles, is his struggle to communicate this essential history of Jesus and of his first witnesses, to which the Christian's understanding of his faith and the Church must always be related, however varied it may be and however different from that of other Christians.

---

rise to a tension in the minds of the gentiles because of their tradition of naturalism or gnostic dualism. This is why Paul had to defend historical salvation against naturalistic misunderstanding."

Translated by David Smith

Henri Irénée Marrou

The Church and
Greek and Roman Civilization

THE appearance and evolution of Christianity have too often been associated with the decline and end of the civilization of the ancient world; Gibbon's *Decline and Fall of the Roman Empire* is characteristic of this tendency. The truth is that Christianity had to contend with "a civilization lacking neither vigour, nor maturity, nor indeed virility".[1] The civilization that Hans Urs von Balthasar was thinking of in this regard was first-century Rome, heir to and representative of the then fully assimilated Hellenistic civilization, which Rome protected and allowed to develop in the East, and implanted and developed in the West, which was either already Latin or coming to be so. Few civilizations have been so self-confident, so conscious of their greatness. The Rome of the time of Augustus and Virgil, i.e., that of the century following the good Antonian emperors, considered itself to be assuming and advancing the civilizing work of Athens: the *Pax Augusta*, the extension everywhere of order, law, an honest administration, and a liberal state which was reducing its military commitments, and therefore its demands, to a minimum. Aelius Aristides wrote that Rome had done as much as Triptolemus for the happiness of humanity and ease of life.[2] Certainly there already were signs of erosion at the end of the second century; and in the third—from 235 to 284, to be exact—the Empire suffered a terrible crisis in which it all but perished; but, thanks to the forceful policies of Diocletian, its history took a new

[1] Hans Urs von Balthasar, *Das Ganze im Fragment.*
[2] Aelius Aristides, *Orat.*, XXVI (Keil, 101).

47

direction: a new type of state was established—an absolute monarchy supported by a powerful administrative apparatus in the sense that has come to be associated with the Russian word *apparat* today. No modern historian any longer thinks of the civilization of late Antiquity as a period of decadence. And the system brought in by Diocletian and perfected by Constantine, even though it succumbed in the West under the onslaught of the barbarian invasions, victoriously prevailed against the decay of centuries: the Roman Empire in the East remained intact until the Arab invasion, and, in the shape of the Byzantine Empire, survived until 1453.

I

"Save yourselves from this crooked generation": these are the words with which Peter brings his first Pentecost sermon to a close (Acts 2. 40). The first generation—the first Christian generations, that is, saw themselves as radically opposed to the "world" (the pejorative connotation given to this word by Christian writers, from Paul and John on, is well known; but it was a word that to pagan ears was redolent of a great number of admirable values) in the sense of the entire circumambient civilization. Of course they did not attack the positive values of that world; the Epistle to the Romans (13. 1–4), for example, in recommending submission to the magistrates, underlines the fact that the man in authority is "God's servant for your good"; but they did affirm the limitation, defects and vices of the existing order: in fact, the environing world seemed to them to be radically tainted in, for example, its cruelties (the gladiatorial combats, or the abandonment of newborn children), its immorality (as recounted in Rom. 1. 24–32), and its idolatry. And by idolatry is meant not only the cult of false gods—the Olympian deities of traditional paganism, or the divinized emperors—but the more profound ignorance of divine reality that was characteristic of this Hellenistic and humane civilization, which might be said to have been too humane in its pursuit of earthly goods, and of the illusory "perfection" denounced by Psalm 119 (118). 96. In fact, even though Christianity at first drew its recruits, statistically speaking, from among the humble, the poor, slaves

and women—the victims of this serenely aristocratic civilization
—it also welcomed representatives of its élite class, whose conversion expressed the dissatisfaction of the satisfied, the answer
to a profound inner demand—for man is a creature oriented to
an absolute. Confronted with this deeply corrupt world, the
Christian Church conceived itself as the new Israel, as the true
people of God, as the community of saints, the called and saved,
those snatched from the powers of darkness (Col. 1. 13), those
who, having received the promise of the Spirit, await the glorious
return of Christ and, with it, their total redemption. The mas-
sive initial failure of Judaeo-Christianity, the lack of response
which Christian preaching first of all met with in pagan circles,
would make obvious the application to the young Church of the
prophetic theology of the "remnant", the privileged subject of
salvation: "And the Lord added to their number day by day
those who were being saved".

Compared with the kingdom of God, what value could the
ephemeral illusion of this world possess? "Render unto
Caesar..." awakened in the first Christians a response which
was very different from that which the theoreticians of medieval
Christianity were to allow it: rather than being a delimitation and
a recognition of temporal power, these words of Jesus' meant for
them: Give back to the master of this world what belongs to
him; get rid of and disclaim these false values. To those who so
often ask (naïvely) whether Jesus and the first Christians were re-
volutionaries, one must reply that for the men of the first century
the political, economic and social structure of the Roman Empire
was something that could not be contested (apart from the exceptional case of the Jewish Zealots, who were terrorists from
whom Jesus—as Cullmann[3] has clearly shown—carefully kept his
distance); for them it was a necessity as inescapable as the laws
of nature. This negative attitude could only be reinforced by the
hope, expectation and conviction that a Parousia was immediately
imminent, that were quite naturally experienced by the first Christians; but it must be emphasized that here a permanent ingredient
of Christianity is evident that was to reappear quasi-periodi-
cally throughout the entire history of the Church. To keep to

[3] O. Cullmann, *Dieu et César*, pp. 11–26; *Jésus et les révolutionaires de
son temps*, pp. 47–80.

4—C.

the ancient world, for us the testimony of a man like Tertullian, who refused any compromise with the pagan world, shows how fully evident in Christian life that attitude still was at the beginning of the third century.

At the same time, one must stress what was equivocal in such a radical position of rejection, and the maintenance of a "pure" stance (to use an expression of A. Labhardt's[4]). Such an attitude of systematic refusal could only have been justified if the second coming of the Lord, and with it the end of history, had almost immediately followed on the first, as the Christians of the first generation showed they hoped by their impatient expectation. It is remarkable that the dangers of such an illusion were already denounced in the Second Epistle to the Thessalonians—the second (in terms of date) of the documents which have been preserved for us in regard to the origins of Christianity: it contains the famous statement (3. 10): "If anyone will not work, let him not eat", the echo of which was to recur right up to and in the Stalinist Constitution of the U.S.S.R. In fact it was not long before the necessities of the human condition were discovered: *necessitates nostrae conversationis*, as it is put in the Latin translation of St Irenaeus.[5] Man is an historical and social being; he is rooted in the civilized environment which moulds him and from which he takes his sustenance. The Christians, too, benefited from the *Pax Romana*: they enjoyed the benefits of the Imperial administration, and the services and comforts assured them by the city governments. In the same passage, St Irenaeus underlines both this fact and the deep reasons for it: "The world is at peace thanks to the Romans; so much so that we are able to travel without fear by land and by sea wherever we will", and further on: "In order to be able to boast of oneself complete separation from pagan society, one would have to possess nothing that came from anyone else, to live completely naked, without shoes or a house, in the mountains and after the fashion of savage beasts. . . ." It was easy, for example, to refuse to do military service by invoking the commandment "Thou shalt not

---

[4] A. Labhardt, "Tertullien et la philosophie ou la recherche d'une 'position pure' ", *Museum Helveticum*, 7 (1950), pp. 159–80.

[5] Ireneaus, *Adv. haer.*, IV, 30, 3 (Massuet; ed. A. Rousseau, *Sources Chrétiennes*, 100, 2, pp. 778–81)

kill . . .", because others, citizens or provincials, took service in the legions, and *auxilia* kept guard against the barbarians! It was easy to retire from public life, because others among the rich pagans argued among themselves for the honour of putting their riches at the service of the common good (municipal finances depended on these voluntary contributions). The difficulties were to become apparent when this liberal system began to show signs of decay, and when social requirements, having become more demanding, threatened the autonomy of individual life: from the end of the second century, the needs of the army became more pressing, and the sons of veterans were enrolled (the *De Corona* of Tertullian bears witness to the dilemmas of conscience that then arose[6]); gradually, the honour of being a member of the *curia* or municipal council became a burden, and soon a crushing one from which those who suffered it could not escape; thus, bit by bit, Christians too were forced to undertake the responsibilities of the civilization that they had wanted, or rather pretended, to be able to reject.

II

"But test everything, hold fast what is good" (1 Thess. 5. 21). The area in which we can study this assumption by Christians of the heritage of Greek and Roman culture is a privileged one: that of intellectual culture. As a religion of the word, Christianity is an intellectual religion. The mission, the proclamation of the good news, imposes on the Church the duty of making itself heard, and understood, which means first of all its own duty of understanding—understanding the content of the message, the sacred books, the basic concepts of revelation. Preaching, exegesis, theology—a whole programme of Christian culture. Was it to be developed from nothing, when classical civilization, then at full maturity, offered Christians its magnificent resources? Admittedly, many of its features were contrary to the gospel ideal: like all of pagan civilization, it was tarnished by idolatry, vanity and error: "See to it that no one makes a prey of you by philosophy and empty deceit" (Col. 2. 8). Here again, at the

[6] Tertullian, *De Cor.*, 1, 1 seq. (ed. J. Fontaine, coll. *Erasme*, 18, pp. 14 ff.).

starting-point, there was reaction and rejection; but as in all other areas, here too it was not easy to refuse to take part. In emerging from its Semitic matrix and accepting a new, Hellenistic formulation, Christianity found itself inserted into a distinct cultural milieu. In a now justly classical observation, Bultmann showed how St Paul was the very first to use the stylistic methods of diatribe and popular pagan philosophy;[7] we have long since become aware that in expressing the Old Testament notion of *Dâbâr* by the term *Logos*, Christian thought was also now located within well-defined conceptual limits—Indo-European, Greek and, in short, philosophical. Certainly the Church has always contained an essential tendency to defy pagan culture which has manifested itself throughout the centuries almost right up to our own times, and which was particularly apparent in ancient times: even at the beginning of the third century, the office of schoolmaster was among the vocations which seemed incompatible with baptism; but it was not very long before the absurdity of this view was realized. The same rigorists (the name of Tertullian recurs here) who refused the Christian the right to teach recognized that it was impossible to keep children away from school—the pagan school. The same Tertullian who emphatically proclaims: *Quid Athenae Hierosolymis* ("What is there in common between Athens and Jerusalem, between the Academy and the Church?"),[8] takes a different tack as soon as he has to attack the heretics, develops a coherent theology, appeals to the very philosophical traditions that he had supposedly rejected, and uses the conceptual material, arguments and method of classical Greek philosophy. Very soon, simultaneously with the rigorist tendency, a more comprehensive attitude developed; already in the middle of the second century, it was neatly formulated by the apologist Justin. Playing—as Clement of Alexandria was to do after him[9]—on the amphiboly divine *Logos*-word, human *Logos*-reason, he explained that all men share in the Word, for

[7] R. Bultmann, *Der Stil der paulinischen Predigt und die zynisch-stoische Diatrib*, in *Forschungen zur Religion und Kultur des Alten und Neuen Testament* 13 (1910).

[8] Tertullian, *De praescr.*, 7, 9 (ed. R. F. Refoulé, *Sources Chrétiennes*, 46, p. 98).

[9] H. I. Marrou, *Introduction à Clement d'Alexandrie: Le Pédagogue*, Book 1 (*Sources Chrétiennes*, 70), pp. 8; 36, n. 8; 46–7.

they all contain a seed of the Logos (literally, *a seed*: Justin makes use of and transposes here the Stoic theory of *Logos spermatikos*); therefore it was far from strange that among the pagans there should be respectable men, philosophers who had at least partly perceived the Truth. How could the Christians hesitate to use what showed itself to be of value in their thinking! "All that they have taught that is good appertains and belongs to us as Christians" (II, *Apol.* 13). It was this attitude that was dominant when from the third century, and even more in the fourth, members of the ruling class of the Empire entered the Church in some number—men who, fully conversant with classical culture, had experienced its merits and knew how to use its resources. But one might really say that the alliance between Christianity and classical culture which was to prove indissoluble later was already firmly sealed from the end of the second century.

Like any human product, this alliance showed itself to be ambivalent. It enriched Western civilization and allowed the magnificent blossoming of classical medieval culture, but we have to ask nowadays whether it did not also obliterate the universalist character of the Christian religion and harm its expansion in other cultures. Even if one restricts one's observations to its manifestations within the still ancient world, its benefits and its dangers appear inextricably mixed. When we read the works of the Fathers of the Golden Age, it is easy to see all that their writings owe in terms of assurance and effectiveness to the perfect mastery that they had acquired in the extraordinarily precise technique that rhetoric had then become; but on the other hand, it is no less evident that very often the Christian preacher had succeeded to the late Sophist lecturer—the "public lecture" had been the most appreciated literary genre among the intellectuals of the Empire in its late, high period—for sacred eloquence had been contaminated by literature (in the pejorative sense): the fourth book of Augustine's *De doctrina Christiana* was to express a necesary reaction to such extremes. Similarly, it is easy for us to recognize all that the thought of Justin or of Hippolytus owes to Stoicism, or indeed the debt owed by Origen to the Platonism of the middle period of that tradition, or that of Gregory of Nyssa or of Augustine to the neo-Platonism of

Plotinus and Porphyry. But recourse to philosophy brought with it deviation or excess: when we try to follow the abstract dialectic by means of which Aetius, the founder of Anomoeanism, tried to show that the term *agen(n)ètos* was an adequate designation of God,[10] we can easily understand how his Cappadocian opponents were able to deplore the fact that in his writings, as in those of his disciple Eunomius, theology had been degraded to the condition of "technology".

III

In the course of the third century, the Church experienced a major demographic and sociological development within the Roman world: all social classes were now represented in the Church, and the various local churches received an often significant fraction of the population, notably in the East. This extension was facilitated by long periods of tranquillity—it is possible to speak even of "the minor peace of the Church"[11]—during which the threat of martyrdom gradually faded in the Christian consciousness. The Church became a mass phenomenon, but at the same time, the quality of its members—statistically speaking—had to suffer. One is not succumbing to pessimism in stating the plain fact that the human species, in view of the ravages of sin, features only a very weak turnover of saints—as of geniuses. The Church no longer received only a small number of élite souls but a very mixed crowd dominated by the mediocre. This can be seen on the morrow of the brief though violent persecutions which marked the middle of the century (Decius 25/1, Valerian 257/8) from the number of *lapsi*, of weak-hearted Christians who had apostatized in the mass in the face of danger, but now hastened to repent and request their readmittance to the Church. The Church could no longer conceive itself as the people of the saints but as a community of sinners on the way to sanctity, an ideal which for

---

[10] Aetius, *Panarion*, III, i, 76 (ed. K. Holl. *Griech. Chr. Schriftsteller*, 37, pp. 351–60 = Athanasius, *Dial. II de ss. Trinitate* (28, cols. 1173–1201).
[11] The expression comes from Walter Pater (*Marius the Epicurean*, ch. 22) who, of course, applies it to the time of Marcus Aurelius, but it is relevant to the third century.

most Christians existed in a very distant perspective! The realization of this transition came about very early in the century, at the time of Pope Callistus (217–222): W. Kamlah has justly spoken of a decisive "turning-point" which occurred then—the "Callistinian turning-point".[12] It was very significant that the Church of Rome chose to put a former banker at its head! It was faced then with serious administrative and financial problems (at the time when it undertook to look after the subterranean cemeteries—the catacombs); but among all the initiative taken by this great pope in very different areas, the one relevant here is his reform of penitential discipline. Until then the Church had considered that three sins were too grave and too contrary to the Christian's vocation to be forgiven; reconciliation of the penitent could take place only at the moment of death; among these three unforgivable sins—homicide, adultery and apostasy—Callistus allows of the second being pardonable. This was a serious decision—it brought violent reactions from the rigorists, right up to schism—which marked the first step along the path that the Church has not strayed from since then—the path of maternal indulgence and understanding of human weakness. That Callistus himself was aware of the implication of his action is clear from the fact (testified to by his opponent Hippolytus[13]) that in order to justify it he had recourse to the parable of the weeds and the wheat: "Let both grow together until the harvest" (Matt. 13. 30). This was a text and an application to be cited and commented upon in the same perspective again and again by the Fathers of the Church—in the case of Africa: Cyprian, St Optatus of Milevis and Augustine. Other comparisons (Noah's ark from Callistus again) and other parables were to be invoked in the same sense: hence we get from Augustine that of the net cast into the sea which brings up all sorts of things, both good and bad, which have to be sorted later; just so, the Church for us is like a huge net which catches all sorts of men, the good who will have to persevere and become better, and the bad who can still change for the better. . . . This was a decisive step forward in the self-understanding of the Church, which henceforth

[12] W. Kamlah, *Christentum und Geschichtlichkeit*, pp. 116–29.
[13] Hippolytus, *Philosophoumena*, IX, 12, 22 (ed. P. Wendland, *Griech. Chr. Schriftsteller*, 26, pp. 249–50).

would conceive itself as a mixed collection dominated still by the sinners, the weak and the mediocre. Thus that equivocation was eliminated which necessarily implied the notion of a community of saints or of the elect: in fact, every time when in the course of Christianity's history, the pretension of a few to form a Church of the pure and perfect reappeared, it was the source of deviations, schisms or heresies which showed its wholly illusory nature.

IV

The history of the Church features a no less decisive "turning-point" with Constantine and his successors. What Tertullian thought of as a radical impossibility occurred: the emperor was converted, and with that the Roman Empire became a Christian Empire. Some persons nowadays are often very severe in regard to the Constantinian and post-Constantinian Church, which has been convicted of compromising itself with the times and of being too well-established in a world which assured its members both honours and prosperity. But one must not commit an anachronism: no more than the first Christians were able to contest the structure of the Empire created by Augustus, were those of the fourth century able to question the existence of an absolute monarchy exercising its authority in all sectors of human life thanks to the communications system of its hierarchical administrative system. From the moment when the sovereign, placed at the summit of this pyramid, became a Christian himself, it was natural that he should put his power at the service of the evangelical ideal, and before all else of the Church as a visible institution, which he favoured by all means, financial contributions, tax exemptions, every kind of privilege for the clergy, and church-building (it was with Constantine, and thanks to him, that the first basilicas appeared). . . . The law tended to adopt the same ideal; hence from 325 there was a law, which certainly emanated (through Constantine) from his Christian advisers, forbidding gladiatorial combat.[14]

Here again we must beware of the sin of anachronism: these interventions of the temporal power in favour of the Church

[14] *Cod. Theodos.*, XV, 12, 1.

must not be interpreted in the light of those that we can observe
in modern states. An emperor of the fourth century is a representative of the "new religiousness", an essentially religious man,
preoccupied before all else with his relations to God. Like his
pagan predecessors, the Christian emperor sees divinity as the
direct source of his power. The Roman Empire saw itself—not
without some illusion—as a universal monarchy; Christian mono-
theism supplied it with what seemed to be a natural interpretation, a theological legitimation. One God, one Logos—and one
emperor as master of the world! The Christian emperor would
necessarily exercise the sovereign power for which he was responsible before God with a view to ensuring as absolute as possible a
Christianization of his empire. In the biography, or rather the
hagiographical elogy, which has been passed down to us as written
by Eusebius, Constantine is given the title of "bishop of the world
without"; it seems that this should be understood in the sense
of "bishop of the men without", the emperor feeling himself
responsible for those among his subjects who were still outside
the fold of the Church. More directly still, he felt himself to be
responsible before God for his Christian subjects; master of the
world after God, it was to him that the task fell of ensuring the
successful running of ecclesiastical institutions. It was the emperor who convoked Councils and presided over them (or had
one of his high functionaries preside over them), who, by a
judicious application of intimidation and of exile, helped ad-
vance the establishment of unanimity, and made sure that decisions taken were put into practice. There is no need to talk
here of Caesaro-papism, a term which is suitable only for
Lutheran Germany or the Russia of Peter the Great: it was the
Church itself which found such interventions quite normal, and
often even solicited them, and rejoiced at them (making only the
reservation that if the emperor turned out to be a heretic, he was
no longer—for those who found him heretical—anything more
than a tyrant and persecutor).

Aided by the example from above, by everything that made
them henceforth so much easier, and also more profitable, con-
versions multiplied. The Christian body grew enormously, and

[15] Eusebius, *Vita Constant.* IV, 24 (ed. I. A. Heikel, *Griech. Chr. Schriftsteller*, 7, p. 126).

tended to represent the majority of the inhabitants of the Empire, and soon their quasi-totality. The Church and Roman society tended to comprise the same human reality, and to become confounded one with the other. This was in fact a second and no less radical turning-point in the self-understanding of the Church. With the Christian Empire (which was to last for centuries in the shape of the Byzantine Empire), there appeared the medieval ideal of sacred Christianity, i.e., that of a society all of whose members, with the exception of small residual minorities, were at least nominally Christian, and all whose institutions, culture and even techniques, therefore submitted to the evangelical ideal and were organized so as to facilitate the realization of such a state of affairs. Here we rediscover the radical ambivalence of all human history, the ambiguity of its creations, the sin, the failure and the sociological and technical burden of the human species. To keep to the above-mentioned example of gladiatorial combat, of murder organized as a spectacle, from which the first Christians had recoiled in horror, the interdiction promulgated in 325 showed itself to be ineffective, inasmuch as it came up against inveterate custom; more than a century more of effort was required before such combats disappeared, towards 434/8, and even then this was the result just as much of economic constraints as of motives of moral order![16]

It must be realized above all that to the extent to which an effort to Christianize the earthly city absorbs energies and preoccupations, it necessarily brings about a reduction of eschatological tension in the Christian consciousness. The anticipation and image, however imperfect and incomplete, that the Christian city offers of the city of God, obscures the image of the city of God and tends to shove desire, hope and expectation into second place. No doubt it is easier for us to excuse the naïve enthusiasm with which the contemporaries of Constantine welcomed the new age: one has only to listen to Eusebius on the subject of the sumptuous banquet given for the bishops by the emperor on the occasion of the Council of Nicaea: "It was undoubtedly an image of the kingdom of Jesus Christ. . . ."[17]—this was on the morrow of the harsh

[16] G. Ville, "Les Jeux de gladiateurs dans l'Empire chrétien", *Mélanges d'Archéologie et d'histoire*, 72 (1960), pp. 273–335.
[17] Eusebius, *Vita. Constant.*, III, 15 (ed. cit., p. 84).

persecutions of Diocletian and Maximian. But the very excessiveness of such propositions reveals by contrast the very real danger which the self-understanding of the Church will always have to reckon with under a regime professing Christianity: that of confounding to some extent the Christian city and the kingdom of God.

V

However, it was at the very moment when Christianity was in this way running the risk of establishing itself far too comfortably in the mode of the times, that a movement arose within the Church which was to maintain itself as living, actual, and actually representative of the pure gospel ideal, without compromise or concessions of any kind. This was the monastic movement. With it there reappeared, in all its strength, the refusal to be limited to the earthly horizon that had so profoundly marked the first Christian generation. What is monasticism if not an effort to realize in full the evangelical counsels: flight from the world, solitude and asceticism appear as the preliminary conditions for a life of prayer, contemplation and familiarity and encounter with God. It is enough here to note the emergence of the movement. In addition, one must remark that monasticism developed within and not without or in opposition to the institutional Church. There is no need to invoke in this regard the antithesis of priesthood and prophetism; there is the collaboration between St Antony, the father of all monks, the prototype of the "charismatic pneumatophore", and St Athanasius, who, by virtue of the very defects of his personality, embodies the very type of the ecclesiastical institution, to stand in evidence. It was at Athanasius' request that Antony left the desert to go to Alexandria in order to help the struggle against the Arians, and it was the same Athanasius who, in writing the famous *Vita Antoni*[18]—the greatest literary success of Christian Antiquity— became the enthusiastic and effective propagandist for the monastic ideal.

In addition, even if the monks did fly the world, the world, or rather the Christians, came to monasticism: "the enthusiasm"

[18] Athanasius, *Vita Antonii*, 26, cols. 837–976.

which animated the monks proved infectious: the sanctity which they attained, the charismata which crowned their endeavours, the sight of this Christianity lived, as whole and heroic, and taken to the extreme of the madness of the Cross, attracted and inspired not only the men and women who came to join the hermits in order to learn from them and become monks or nuns in their turn, but the simple faithful whose vocation kept them within the orbit of family and contemporary life. Many pilgrims went to the desert for edification, to profit from the advice and the spiritual direction of the saintly individuals they met there; but there were many more who by reading or listening were influenced by them. The presence of the monks within the Christian community acted from the beginning, and will always act, as a yeast, as a model and a challenge, and will never allow the salt of the earth to lose its savour or the light of the world to be dimmed within the Church.

Translated by John Griffiths

Georg Denzler

Basic Ecclesiological Structures in the Byzantine Empire

THE Orthodox theologian, Jean Meyendorff, maintains that no distinctively Byzantine ecclesiology was produced between the ninth and the fifteenth centuries: "The Orthodox Church consciously refused to find a synthesis between philosophy and revelation similar to scholasticism in the West, and preferred to go on thinking in patristic categories. Its theology and its doctrine of the sacraments and the Church were never formulated within the framework of a definite philosophy and its structure never became merged with the laws of a definite institution."[1]

Does this mean that ecclesiology played no part in the countless controversies between Rome and Constantinople? We know that, in the main, they were about dogmatic questions (the Holy Spirit, purgatory and so on), liturgy (unleavened bread in the Eucharist and the *epiclesis*) and Church discipline (such as priestly celibacy and fasting on Saturday). We also know that many of the Orthodox answers to these and similar questions revealed a very distinctive understanding of the essence and the task of the Church.[2] For example, one party accorded to

---

[1] J. Meyendorff, *Die orthodoxe Kirche gestern und heute* (Series Wort und Antwort 31) (Salzburg, 1963), pp. 256–7; translated from the French, *L'Église orthodoxe hier et aujourd'hui* (Paris, 1960).

[2] The most important sources will be found in M. Jugie, *Theologia dogmatica christianorum orientalium ab ecclesia catholica dissidentium* IV (Paris, 1931), pp. 203–642 (*Tractatus de ecclesia*). W. de Vries has for years been investigating the structure of the Church in the light of the ecumenical councils of the first ten centuries A.D. See, for example, his recent article "Die Struktur der Kirche gemäss dem Konzil von Chalkedon

conciliar canons the status of a supreme decision, whereas their opponents expected the ultimate decision from the pope. This, of course, was the most delicate point of all in the different ways in which the Church was viewed in the East and in the West. We must, however, first consider the question of ecclesiology in the East on a broader basis.

I. Names for the Church

What the Fathers of the First Council of Nicaea (A.D. 325) meant when they called the Church *catholica et apostolica ecclesia* was the totality of those who believed in the Trinity. The Council of Constantinople (381) professed faith in *unam catholicam et apostolicam ecclesiam*, in which the attributes "catholic" and "apostolic" could apply both to a part of the Church and to the sum total of all parts of the Church which went back to one apostle.

The imperial "State Church" policy, however, resulted in a "Roman consciousness" coming about in the Church and in the concepts "Roman" and "Catholic" becoming equivalents. There was an increasing tendency in the Roman curia by the seventh century to confine the whole of the *universalis ecclesia* to the *romana ecclesia*, that is, to the Latin Church. Ideologically, these tendencies were very closely connected with a consistently

---

(451)", in *Orientalia christiana periodica* 35 (1969), pp. 63-122. Y. Congar has also contributed a very instructive study on this subject—*L'ecclésiologie du haut moyen âge. De Saint Grégoire le Grand à la désunion entre Byzance et Rome* (Paris, 1968), pp. 319-93 (L'Orient. Accord et divergences ecclésiologiques avec Rome et l'Occident). Apart from these three contributions, the following works must be mentioned: G. Ostrogorsky, *Geschichte des byzantinischen Staates* (Munich, ²1952); A. Michel, *Die Kaisermacht in der Ostkirche 843-1204* (Darmstadt, 1959); H.-G. Beck, *Kirche und theologische Literatur im byzantinischen Reich* (Byzantinisches Handbuch im Rahmen des Handbuchs der Altertumswissenschaft II/1) (Munich, 1959); Panagiotis Bratsiotis (ed.), *Die orthodoxe Kirche in griechischer Sicht*, 2 volumes (Die Kirchen der Welt, I) (Stuttgart, 1959-1960); B. Bobrinskoy, O. Clément, B. Fize and J. Meyendorff (eds.), *Der Primat des Petrus in der orthodoxen Kirche* (Bibliothek für orthodoxe Theologie und Kirche I) (Zürich, 1961)—see especially the contributions by N. Afanassieff, N. Koulomzine, J. Meyendorff and A. Schmemann; W. de Vries, *Orthodoxie und Katholizismus. Gegensatz oder Ergänzung?* (Freiburg, 1965); see also J. Meyendorff, *op. cit.*

effected policy of stressing the central importance, both in theory and in practice, of the *Cathedra Petri* in Rome. Despite the increasing number of differences in tradition and organization between the two Church communities, the term *catholica ecclesia* occurs again and again in the letter of Pope Leo IX († 1054), whose main concern was for the unity of the Church, as a common title for both communities. This at the same time undeniably presupposed the pre-eminence of the bishop of Rome.

The word "orthodox", which, of course, related in the first place to faith, was also applied to the whole Church. The Second Ecumenical Council, at Constantinople (381), was officially the "Sacred Synod of Orthodox Bishops". The Church of the Patriarchate of Constantinople also had the title of "Orthodox Eastern Church". It was not, however, until the sixteenth century that the word "orthodox" came to be used exclusively for the Eastern Churches.[3]

The national Churches which had arisen in protest against the Christological dogma defined at Chalcedon (451)—the Palestinian and Syrian Churches—were at first known as the *orientalis ecclesia*, but, by the end of the first millennium, the terms "Oriental Church" and "Orthodox Church" were applied to all the Churches in the East, but above all to the Church of the Byzantine Empire. From this time onwards, the two terms *orientalis ecclesia* and *occidentalis ecclesia* were placed in antithesis.

II. THE CHURCH AS A MYSTERY

In Orthodox theology, the divinity of Christ and the divine aspect of the Church were strongly stressed and the biblical concept of the "body of Christ" became the commonest name for the Church. This came about in the following way. Christ, the universal head of the Church, filled all the members of the body with a life that was regarded as a mystical reality which, in the view of John Damascene († ca. 750), permeated the whole life of the Christian. The Church's main function—to sanctify men —was, according to Cyril of Jerusalem († 387), accomplished

---

[3] See M. Sesan, " 'Orthodoxie'. Histoire d'un mot et de sa signification", in *Istina* (1970), pp. 425–34.

by the Holy Spirit, who never became obscured in the Eastern Church.

Man's sanctification took place above all in the celebration of the mysteries of baptism and the eucharist. According to Maximus Confessor († 662) and John Damascene, the eucharist established a living contact with God through Christ and with one's fellow men. Since, however, not only Christians living in faith on earth, but also those who had died and gone beyond faith to a vision of the divine mystery, belonged to the "communion of saints", or the Church, a fifteenth-century Orthodox theologian could regard the eucharist as a "communal meal in heaven and on earth, one eucharist and one blessedness".[4]

Although there was considerable agreement between East and West as to the Church as a mystery, as a sacramental or mystical reality, it is undeniable that the Western Church moved more and more towards legalism, whereas the Greek Church thought of itself increasingly as a spiritual community. This different emphasis led inevitably to tension and eventually to schism.

III. THE CHURCH AS A VISIBLE COMMUNITY

The Byzantine theologians were primarily concerned with the inner life of the Church, stressing above all the activity of the Spirit in the mysteries celebrated by the priest, and the necessity of membership of the visible Church (Origen, † ca. 254, Cyprian of Carthage, † ca. 258, Basil the Great, † ca. 459).

1. Bible, Tradition and Hierarchy

In this, they regarded tradition as almost as important as the Bible. The dogmatic decisions of the first seven ecumenical councils, and especially the Nicene-Constantinopolitan creed, were for them unchangeable tradition in the narrower sense. Tradition in the broader sense of less essential doctrines, liturgy and so on, also played an important part in the life of the Church. Emperor Justinian I († 565) believed that "the faithful retention of the tradition left to us by the apostles... and protected and

---

[4] Quoted by Congar in *L'ecclésiologie, op. cit.*, p. 339, note 60.

explained by the Fathers"[5] was the best safeguard of peaceful government.

In the East and in the West, Scripture and tradition were seen as the only ways to keep the apostolic inheritance intact; what really formed part of that tradition was the concern of the hierarchy—the bishops who had been appointed in apostolic succession were in communion with each other and were responsible in synod for deciding about questions of faith.

2. Synod, Council and Pentarchy

From the middle of the second century onwards, bishops from many dioceses were gathering in synod in Antioch, Alexandria and Constantinople. Supreme authority was accorded to the ecumenical councils, at which the emperor usually exercised a decisive influence.

After Constantine († 337) had moved his residence from Rome to Byzantium, the bishop there tried to achieve priority for his church. The First Council of Constantinople (381) gave him a position immediately below that of the bishop of Rome and, mainly for political reasons, the Council of Chalcedon (451) confirmed the precedence of Constantinople over Antioch and Alexandria. This order of preference (canon 28) was rejected later by Pope Leo I as contradictory to tradition.

The Fourth Ecumenical Council of Constantinople (869–870) approved the pentarchy, or government by five patriarchs in the order Rome, Constantinople, Alexandria, Antioch, Jerusalem. The leading position of the Roman patriarch or pope in all questions except the exercise of universal legal authority was accepted by all. Rome, however, soon began to apply this patriarchal principle to achieve her own ends.

In the Orthodox Church, the acceptance of a dogma by the whole Christian community played an important part in its definition as infallibe. When Byzantine theologians considered the Church, what they had in mind firstly was a concrete local community led by a bishop, and only secondly the unity of the various communities, which they saw less as a legal bond and more as a mystical union with the body of Christ. This, they

[5] H. Rahner, *Kirche und Staat im frühen Christentum. Dokumente aus acht Jahrhunderten und ihre Deutung* (Munich, 1961), p. 299.

believed, had to be realized in the "communion of the Churches", fundamentally established in the conciliar definitions and creeds.

In the West, on the other hand, the importance of the local churches declined as that of the universal Church rose. They became regarded simply as parts of the whole—a whole increasingly governed, not synodally, but monarchically, by the pope. This tendency was, however, matched in the East, where the Byzantine patriarch was often a very strong personality who overshadowed his Eastern colleagues and even earned for Constantinople the title of "mother of all the other Churches" (including the Western Church).

3. State, Emperor and Imperial Church

At the end of the fourth century, Christianity became the State religion and the expanding Christian community in the Byzantine Empire was led by two hiararchies—that of the Church with the patriarch at its summit and that of the state headed by the emperor, who also played a decisive part in the life of the Church. "Both the character of this State and the emperor towards the Church can be understood in the light of Constantine's relationship with the Church."[6] The emperor's rule was seen as the emanation of divine power, he was venerated as the representative of God and as an apostle, his office was acknowledged by Pope Leo I as priestly and he was regarded as competent to judge in matters of faith. The "priest-emperor" Justinian was supremely aware of the pre-eminent position and the so-called "nomocanons" with legal validity guaranteed by both Church and State are clear proof of the close liaison between the two powers.

Although the emperor's direct power did not extend to dogmatic decisions, he did summon, preside over and direct the proceedings of synods and councils and give their decrees the force of law in the Empire. In the same way, the Church was not separate from the State, but was seen as an aspect of the one

[6] See O. Treitinger, *Die oströmische Kaiser- und Reichsidee. Nach ihrer Gestaltung im höfischen Zeremoniell* (Jena, 1858), p. 220; reprinted Darmstadt, 1956.

Christian society, a part of the Empire governed by God's anointed.

In the East, Church and State sometimes opposed and sometimes co-operated with each other. During the first thousand years of Christianity, the emperor to a very great extent ruled the Church. From the middle of the eleventh century, however, his power decreased. Patriarch Cerularius († 1058) fought strenuously for the separation of Church and State, arguing that it was his task to guide the Church and the emperor's to govern the State. He even wore imperial purple shoes and threatened to depose the emperor if the dividing line was crossed. This duel ended with the defeat of both parties. Shortly afterwards, the emperor's privileged position was undermined by being traced back, not to a divine right, but simply to a concession granted by the Church.

All the same, despite these and other changes, the Byzantine understanding of the Church continued to be based essentially on the idea that the emperor played a decisive part in the "imperial" Church.

4. *Peter, the Pope and the Primacy of Faith*

The Orthodox theologians never doubted the pre-eminence of Peter among the apostles, but they confined the function of rock and bearer of the keys (Matt. 16. 18) exclusively to him and never applied it to the bishop of Rome, with the result that the latter was never thought of as Peter continuing to live and to exercise full power in the Church. As the patriarch of the West, the bishop of Rome was regarded as the arbitrator in cases where canon law was disputed, but the task of making dogmatic decisions was reserved for the ecumenical councils. During the patriarchates of Photius and Cerularius especially, the Byzantine Church unswervingly opposed any theory or practice that might lead to the primacy of the pope in jurisdictional matters, to any infallibility in questions of dogma, or to a centralization of Church government by the pope. The leaders of the Eastern Church insisted much more on the autonomy of the separate dioceses and local churches. It was only because of the political status of his residence in Constantinople that the patriarch of

that city enjoyed an "honorary" primacy which was never precisely defined.

The gulf between Rome and Byzantium became too wide to
bridge when the view put forward by Nicholas I († 867) and so
many of his successors became widely accepted in the West.
This pope claimed a *plenitudo potestatis* over all the Western
and Eastern Churches, and later, in 1053, Leo IX affirmed that
the holy Roman and apostolic see was, according to the Lord
Jesus, the "head" of all God's Churches.[7] At this time, too, the
name "mother" was often applied to the Roman Church.

This different attitude towards the question of primacy resulted in the Latin and Greek Churches going their own way
more and more. Occasional dialogues and even the Unions of
Lyons (1274) and Florence (1439) did not reduce the tension.
On neither side did the clergy and the people really desire reunion, nor were they in any sense prepared for it. Two such
divergent theologies had been developed on both sides that any
merging of the two seemed out of the question.

The main reason for the schism between East and West was,
in the view of most eminent theologians over several centuries,
that dogmatic decisions were made in the Latin Church by the
pope, but in the Greek Church by the councils. In his treatise on
the "causes of the dogmatic differences in the Church", the
Orthodox theologian Nicholas Cabasilas († ca. 1363) clearly outlined the Eastern attitude: "It is not, as the Roman Church in-
sists, that we claim primacy and cannot agree to take second
place after Rome. We have never quarrelled with the Roman
Church about primacy, and there is no question here about taking second place. We know the ancient practice of the Church
and the decrees of the Fathers, who called the Roman Church
the oldest of all the Churches. . . . What, then, is the cause of
this disagreement? It is that this controversial question has not
been resolved by a communal decision on the part of an ecumenical council, and that it has not been settled on the basis of the
ancient practice of the Fathers of the Church, but that the
Romans have been playing the part of the master in this and

[7] C. Will, *Acta et scripta quae de controversiis ecclesiae graecae et latinae
extant* (Leipzig and Marburg, 1861), p. 71; reprinted Frankfurt a.M.,
1963.

have treated the others like obedient schoolboys."[8] Another Orthodox theologian, Simeon of Thessalonica († 1429), was prepared to accept the pope's claim to supreme authority if this was backed by the faith of Peter, saying that Peter could only be regarded as the rock because he had confessed faith in the Son of God.[9]

Despite an underlying agreement about the inner essence of the community of Jesus, these two radically different ways of interpreting the Petrine office led firstly to divergent views concerning the structure of the Church, and secondly to schism, even though no exact date can be given for the beginning of that schism.[10] We are bound to conclude, then, that, instead of safeguarding the unity of Christianity, the office of Peter was the cause of disunity.

[8] Migne, *Patrologia graeca*, 149, 685.
[9] *Expositio sancti symboli*, *Patrologia graeca*, 155, 795; *Dialogus in Christ—adversus omnes haereses*, ibid., 119.
[10] See G. Denzler, "Das sogannte morgenländische Schisma im Jahre 1054", in *Münchener Theologische Zeitschrift* 17 (1966), pp 24–46; *ibid.*, "Das morgenländische Kirchenschisma im Verständnis von Päpsten und Ökumenischen Konzilien des Mittelalters", in *Münchener Theologische Zeitschrift* 20 (1969), pp. 104–17; Y. Congar, "Quatre siècles de désunion et d'affrontement. Comment Grecs et Latins se sont appréciés réciproquement au point de vue ecclésiologique", in *Istina* (1968), pp. 131–52.

Translated by David Smith

August Nitschke

The Church of God as the Dominant Power in Europe

THE Church has always been, as it were, a stranger in the midst of other human communities, because it has, so its members believe, "a visible and an invisible aspect, a terrestrial and a heavenly mode of existence". Its development is based on human decisions which have been "given by the Holy Spirit". In an attempt to define its unique character, it has been called the "body of Christ", and later the "mystical body" (*corpus mysti-cum*).[1]

As an institution subject to all the laws to which all human institutions are bound to submit, the Church claimed that it was at the same time a supraterrestrial institution, created by God and maintained by him. This claim inevitably led to great tensions between the Church and society, tensions which have never in the course of history been greater than in the period between the seventh and the thirteenth centuries. This was the period (the pontificates of Gregory VII and Innocent III, for example) when Church leaders won enormous political power over a united European empire of many different peoples with Latin as the one official language. The astonishing influence of the Church on people's lives is reflected in the glory of the medieval churches, which were often far more splendid than the homes

---

[1] See R. Snackenburg, "Kirche", in *Lexikon für Theologie und Kirche*, 6 (1961), p. 172; J. Ratzinger, *ibid.*, p. 177; G. le Bras, *Sociologie de l'église dans le haut moyen âge* (Le Chiese, Settimane di Studio del Centro Italiano, 7), Spoleto (1960), pp. 595 ff.; H. de Lubac, *Corpus mysticum* (Paris, ²1949).

of the nobles, who preferred to spend their wealth on church buildings.

People were convinced not only that the Church and its decrees were directly guided by God, but also that worldly, political decisions were ultimately made by him. How, the Church historian is bound to ask, did this conviction that an obviously terrestrial institution such as the Church had a supraterrestrial origin and supraterrestrial power come about especially at a time when the terrestrial, secular power of the Church was so enormous? Church historians have put forward many different explanations, three of which are particularly striking.

The first is that the ruling classes appealed to God in an attempt to justify their power. The second is that these ruling powers followed essentially religious ideas. The third is that medieval men had a very special experience of being directly dependent on God, and that this experience led them to assume without question that the institutions of society were also directly subject to God's will.

I. God's Will claimed by Rival Groups

Since the Enlightenment at least, there has been an inclination to interpret religious propositions as ideological statements. This conviction had helped men to gain power and then to justify their action. As Voltaire said, "priests' oracles, miracles and intrigues" had determined the fate of men; and Marx and Engels, in the same vein, said that the clergy "represented the ideology of medieval feudalism". Many modern sociologists have expressed a similar view: i.e., that priests claimed that their power was directly derived from God's will, and that they preserved people's faith in order to exercise that power.[2]

This explanation cannot be taken seriously today, mainly because it omits the changes that took place in the Church during the period under consideration. The Church was dominated until the early eleventh century, not by priests, but by noblemen, and later by a group of monks and clergy. After the twelfth century,

---

[2] *Oeuvres complètes de Voltaire*, ed. Moland (Paris, 1878–1885), XIX, p. 354; F. Engels, *The German Peasants' War* (K. Marx, F. Engels, *Werke* 7, Berlin, 1964, p. 334).

the dominant force consisted of university-educated jurists and theologians.

Another version of this theory has been put forward: the nobles claimed supremacy on the basis of a pre-Christian, Germanic, conviction that they were the direct descendants of gods and therefore possessed special magic powers which guaranteed their leading position. On the one hand, these Christianized nobles interpreted Christian teaching in this pre-Christian sense, making Jesus, for example, a liege-lord, while, on the other hand, the Church had to accept their rule.

From about the middle of the eleventh century onwards, however, certain monks and priests came to power by disputing that the nobles enjoyed any special privilege by right of birth, and by claiming that they, as men who had turned away from the world to serve their fellow men, should possess power. Reforming popes such as Gregory VII, and monks such as Bernard of Clairvaux, are outstanding examples of this movement.

According to this theory of history, the rule of the monks and priests was followed by that of university-educated theologians and jurists, who claimed that God had given them powers to pass judgment, as he did, on good and evil and on men's sins. Alexander III, Innocents III and IV and Boniface VIII were typical of this kind of ruler. From the thirteenth century onwards, too, the emerging middle classes began to struggle for supremacy over the mendicant orders.[3]

In the opinion of these historians, then, each successive group in power in the Middle Ages insisted that the Church was a divinely created institution, in order to gain, maintain, improve and justify its position of power.

II. Prevailing Ideas of the Political Freedom of the Church

The second explanation put forward is that there are certain

[3] W. Groenbech, *Vor Folkeaert i Oltiden* (Copenhagen, 1909–1912); in German: *Kultur und Religion der Germanen* (Darmstadt, 1961); F. Kern, *Gottesgnadentum und Widerstandsrecht im früheren Mittelalter* (Leipzig, 1914); M. Maccarrone, "Vicarius Christi: Storia del titolo papale", in *Lateranum* 18 (1952); F. Kempf, "Papsttum und Kaisertum bei Innozenz III", in *Misc. Hist. Pont.* 19 (Rome, 1954); H. Grundmann, *Religiöse Bewegungen im Mittelalter* (Hildesheim, 1961).

ideas about the Church that have changed in the Church, and others that have persisted throughout the passage of time. Man's idea of the Church is both static and dynamic. Historians of this school have suggested that, in the earliest Christian centuries, Paul's idea of the body of Christ and Augustine's doctrine of the kingdom of God predominated in all thinking about the Church. In the twelfth century, there was an enrichment by ideas drawn from later classical antiquity and by a revived interest in Roman law and Aristotelian philosophy. All these developments helped to change the idea of the Church as an organization. On the other hand, there has been a persistent conviction, which originally goes back to the New Testament, that the Church is a community founded and kept in being by God.[4]

One of the ideas about the Church which has emerged more clearly, and has been increasingly put into practice in the course of time, is that "something of Christ's supraterrestrial freedom has penetrated into the visible Church" and that this freedom has been interpreted more and more as a political freedom of the Church, as *libertas Ecclesiae*. One of the Church leaders who fought to achieve this freedom was Gregory VII, who has, for this reason, been called "fanatically insistent on an idea" and "rigidly and unswervingly convinced of its divine legality".[5]

According to other historians, leaders of the medieval Church tried to apply the idea of the "pre-eminence of the Roman Church", thus revealing as an ideology their conviction that papal authority embraced both the spiritual sphere and the sphere of secular government. One Church historian has declared that it was his aim to provide the history of the gradual emergence of an idea, without passing judgment on its historical or metahistorical origin.[6] But the origin of this idea was theological, and therefore combined "a terrestrial and a heavenly mode of existence".

[4] E. H. Kantorowicz, *The King's Two Bodies—A Study in Mediaeval Political Theory* (Princeton, 1957).
[5] G. Tellenbach, *Libertas, Kirche und Weltordnung im Zeitalter des Investiturstreites* (Stuttgart, 1936); H. Grundmann, "Das Hohe Mittelalter und die deutsche Kaiserzeit", *Neue Propyläen-Weltgeschichte* 2 (1940), p. 248.
[6] W. Ullmann, *The Growth of Papal Government in the Middle Ages* (London, 1955).

III. The Experience of Man's Freedom in Dependence on God

The third explanation is that of the historians who base their conclusions on human experience. According to one group of such historians, specifically Christian experiences have taken place when believers, in imitation of Christ, have tried to live in accordance with New Testament teaching.

The earliest stage in this history of the imitation of Christ was that of the monks of the school of St Anthony, who took Jesus' lonely fight against temptation in the desert as their model. Later, as well as living as hermits, monks fought against evil in communities, at the same time praising God (as the Benedictine communities did) in their shared liturgy. Special experiences were common to all these monks: that of victory over sin and temptation, and that of service to a victorious ruler. These experiences resulted in a conviction that God helped them to victory in their struggle.

From the mid-eleventh century onwards, another experience resulted from a further stage in this evangelical imitation of Christ: that of the itinerant, communal "apostolic life" of preaching, teaching and pastoral work in accordance with the example given by Jesus and his apostles. The love shown by the Augustinian, Premonstratensian and other canons was derived, they believed, directly from God's love.

A further stage was reached in the thirteenth century, when Franciscan and other mendicant friars began to follow Jesus in his renunciation of all worldly possessions. These poor beggars were convinced that their experience of love for Christ had been awakened in them by God himself.[7]

New Testament teachings were practised in all these different ways of imitating Christ, and the result was an experience of being directly guided by God. This in turn resulted in a conviction that those who belonged to the Church—as, indeed, the Church itself —were directly influenced by God.

The historians of the second group are not primarily concerned

[7] M. Heimbucher, *Die Orden und Kongregationen der katholischen Kirche* 2 (Paderborn, 1933-1934); A. Nitschke, "Die Wirksamkeit Gottes in der Welt Gregors VII", in *Studi Gregoriani* 5 (1956), pp. 115 ff.; *ibid.*, *Heilige in dieser Welt* (Stuttgart, 1962)

with specifically *Christian* experience, but with man's experience of a special kind of freedom which, throughout history, has enabled him to feel very closely associated with one aspect of the phenomena which surround him. This experience of freedom, or "homogeneity", makes some men feel that their actions are entirely in accordance with those phenomena, and that this has a strong impact on the way in which they perceive phenomena.

It is remarkable that this experience of freedom, or "homogeneity", was exactly the same as the Christian religious experience in the period in question. This was not the case in other periods.

In the ancient world, most men felt they were slaves of their own bodies and only free when they controlled their more "lowly" parts. They were always, however, bound to their more "noble" parts, and tended to perceive bodies or isolated groups of bodies everywhere. Since the Renaissance, on the other hand, men have felt that they were part of a three-dimensional space and were only free when they could develop within this space. They have felt bound to a "force" which makes this free development—or at least movement in space—possible. Post-Renaissance men have tended, as their paintings so clearly show, above all to represent a space, into which phenomena are fitted.

Medieval men, unlike men in the ancient and in the post-Renaissance world, did not perceive themselves and their environment as individual groups of bodies or as parts of a three-dimensional space, but as closely interrelated with every other person and every other being. This again is clearly demonstrated in the painting, sculpture and architecture of the Middle Ages, in which no figure is isolated or simply a part of a three-dimensional space, but in which everything is interrelated. One consequence of this way of perceiving things was the structure of medieval government, which took the form of a personal relationship, one person being orientated to another person, and bound to him in faithfulness or fealty, by some other form of dependence.

How did men experience freedom in the Middle Ages? Not in controlling their more "lowly" bodily parts, or in developing their own persons, or achieving free movement in space, but rather in a situation in which two intimately related persons confronted each other, in which one man was dependent on another, more powerful person. The man who was dependent on the most powerful person was most free. This rule also applied in the political sphere, in which princes and cities of the Holy Roman Empire, directly dependent on the emperor, had greater freedom than all other princes and cities. In the religious sphere, those who were directly subject to the pope had the greatest freedom. Those who subordinated themselves directly to the most powerful being of all, God, had the greatest freedom of all. In this way, medieval man's experience of freedom was a religious experience, an experience of God himself. It is now possible for us to understand how a human institution, the Church, could at the same time be experienced as divine.

IV. Man's Changing Experience of Freedom and Changes in the Church

We can follow the changes in the Church by following the changes in man's experience of freedom. From the seventh until the eleventh century, the free man was the man whose strength was derived from someone more powerful than himself—a strength which defined his actions and which above all enabled him to achieve victory. In the tenth century, this led to the supremacy of the nobility. The same strength, however, could also lead to activity on behalf of other men; and in the eleventh century, this brought about the supremacy of the monks and priests, and of the reforming popes, such as Gregory VII, and ultimately the great struggle between spiritual and secular power.

In the twelfth and thirteenth centuries, the free man was very often a judge who was able to strengthen or tone down the natural dispositions of other men; this led to the supremacy of governing jurists who believed that, like God who was supremely powerful, they could change men, because they shared in the divine nature. The secular rulers and the popes of this period possessed this freedom, and inevitably they came into conflict with each other (the second great struggle for power) because both sides claimed divine right.

From the thirteenth century onwards, the man who turned towards perfection in a realization of his own shortcomings was free. Although this was once again a relationship between two persons, greater emphasis was placed in man's efforts and it was clearly acknowledged that the highest perfection was that of God, to whom all man's activities were directly related.

All these different experiences of freedom had their impact on man's perception of reality. They were reflected in the art and architecture of the various periods, in human behaviour, and in public and legal institutions.[8] It must be stressed that in all this freedom was always directly related to God, with the result that men almost automatically chose to live in communities created and kept in existence by God.

V. Conclusion: Different Historical Interpretations

What can be learnt from the history of the Church in the Middle Ages? We have very briefly considered several different historical interpretations, some from the Christian point of view, other not specifically Christian. Even historians who approach the problem in the light of a Christian understanding may reach different conclusions: for example, that the history of the Church was determined by an ideology, or that it was the result of experiences gained by imitating Christ.

On the other hand, the conclusions of historians whose approach is not explicitly Christian can also differ widely. In this sense, their findings are parallel to those of specifically Christian historians. One scholar, for example, may be convinced of a struggle for power between rival social groups, each seeking to justify an ideology. Another may attribute historical change to a change in man's perception of reality and trace this back to certain experiences of freedom. In that case, he cannot deny that the freedom of medieval man was directly based on his dependence on God. He is bound to regard the great importance of the Church in the Middle Ages as the sign of medieval man's constant turning towards freedom, and of his acquisition—through achieving this true freedom—of an appropriate means of perceiving reality. We may therefore conclude that any study of Church history provides us with a norm which we can apply to ourselves.

[8] A. Nitschke, *Naturerkenntnis und politisches Handeln im Mittelalter: Körper-Bewegung-Raum* (Stuttgart, 1967).

Translated by David Smith

Bernard Plongeron

Archetypal Christianity: the Models of 1770 and 1830

I SHALL define my terms by quoting Mircea Eliade's remarks on archetypes and repetitions: "In the primitive mind, the old time consisted of the profane succession of all the events without meaning, events, that is, with no archetypal models; 'history' is the remembrance of those events, of what can only really be called 'unmeanings' or even 'sins' (inasmuch as they are divergences from the archetypal norms).... The repetition shows the paradoxical wish to achieve an ideal form (the archetype) in the very framework of human existence, to be in time without reaping its disadvantages, without the inability to 'put back the clock'."[1]

Such would seem to be the problem which confronted the Church of the *Ancien Régime* in its dialectical agony between its heavy temporal commitments and its eschatological ultimate. The stroke of genius—since Gregory VII, if not Constantine—had certainly consisted in bringing a certain harmony to the whole endeavour by transposing temporal duration and profane values into a kind of Christian time which subjected men and their institutions to the idea of an extra-temporal salvation which only the Church possessed the key to. Thus there evolved the archetype of a "Christianity" immersed in the Scholastic universe, from the thirteenth century to classical Europe, all the more capable of maintaining the archetypal fiction since (as

[1] M. Eliade, *Patterns in Comparative Religion* (London, 1958), pp. 401, 408.

78

Pierre Chaunu remarks[2]) human and economic techniques had not changed notably in the interval of three or four centuries. But, suddenly, with the turning-point of the 1770s, not only Europe but the Atlantic world burst the bonds of Christianity. Was this just a passing madness, this sudden ferment of intellectual and economic changes, this revolutionary whirlwind which affected the old European countries and the young America in a kind of chain reaction between 1762 and 1789? Sunk in its Christian reverie, the Church—at least that of the pope, the bishops and the supposedly orthodox theologians—took it to be just such a transient phenomenon. When the troublemakers of this "philosophy" of enlightenment referred to the frustrations of the Renaissance, the official Church smiled understandingly. Surely it had nipped in the bud and destroyed once and for all the demons of modernity of the sixteenth century? Had it not reduced the fever of creative energy that it, the Church, called the "diabolical pride of human reason", to such an extent that (as Henri Hauser puts it), after that tumult, "Europe seemed so tired of having lived so hectically that it turned in on itself and looked back to the past"?[3] The Church's tactics had allowed the Council of Trent, by means of its disciplinary and even sacramental canons, definitively to mould ecclesiastical structures into State structures—the new concept that the old Christianity agreed to recognize in the modern world. This concession was all the more profitable, inasmuch as the sacralization of monarchical power constituted the ordered society at the head of which was the clergy, whose sociological empire emerged confirmed and reinforced.

With its temporal domination renewed, the spiritual Church could only use some of the weapons of "Christianity" to anathematize all those who contested the pyramidal and feudal structure of politico-religious society. To the voices of protest from without —the "unbeliever", the "atheist", the "protestant" and even the "pagan"—the Church answered sharply: Outside the Church there is no salvation! Outside this Church privileged to control human governments according to the divine norms entrusted to

[2] P. Chaunu, *La civilisation de l'Europe Classique* (Paris, 1966), pp. 26-28.

[3] H. Hauser, *La modernité du XVIe siècle* (Paris, 1963), p. 65.

the keepers of its sacred books. This calm assurance had only just been disturbed when, having fired the anticlerical broadsides of the *Encyclopédie*, the "philosophers" brought their deadliest artillery to bear on the Church: was not salvation, the image of Christian happiness, just an evasion of the conditions necessary for a civilization of human happiness demanded by all the classes of an enlightened society? A major debate that would affect the future of the Church and the world; a problem to mobilize the theologians; but there were only apologists ready to deploy their talents and defeat this badly posed question.

It is easy to reproach them for their internal contradictions, and their own divergences of thought on the subject,[4] when they tried to prove the social compatibility of Christianity. Some Christians, indeed, did inform them that they would be more convincing if they stopped savouring their Tridentine triumph and busied themselves with representing the Church in another sort of way. These Gallicans, Josephites, Jansenists, Febronianists and Presbyterians held out for a Church that would no longer sanctify a society founded on inequality, and which would renew its fidelity to the apostolic age, to that of Cyprian and Augustine—whom they continually cited.

With its claim to Christianity thus impugned, the Church spent its energy on an inquisitorial process whose real beneficiaries were kings and parliaments. It forced Christians into a subversion that was more theological than political, enclosed itself in its own debates, and merely reinforced its conventional response to the "obdurate souls" who continued to ask their major question. Why did the Church not give a proper answer?

Within the space available here, I can only refer to two aspects of the question which became intermingled and remained apparent with unusual consistency from 1770 to 1830: on the one hand, the ambiguity of the debate; on the other, its consequences for Christian life. Undoubtedly, at the moment when the

---

[4] Some Jansenists like Mesenguy (*Exposition de la religion chrétienne, 3e entretien, Du bonheur de l'homme et de la verité de la religion chrétienne*, vol. I, 1774) defended the compatibility of human happiness and Christian happiness when the Ultramontanes introduced a radical division: the Jesuit Croiset (*Réflexions chrétiennes sur divers sujets de morale*, vol. II, 1743) and the famous Abbé Bergier (1718–90), followed mainly by Cardinal Gerdil and Adeodato Turchi, the "Italian Massillon".

unified Catholic consciousness suffered the pluralistic attack of the Enlightenment, the problem of the Church and that of "religion" should have been dissociated but were to be permanently confused by intra- and extra-Christian polemics. The first conditioned the second, and Catholicism laid itself open to losing the philosophical battle which at the beginning of the nineteenth century centred upon the concept of religion; it put itself in this position because it had not previously resolved its ecclesiological difficulties. Both required a rigorous application of dogmatic thought, the absence of which not only risked a total absence of clarity but the belief, from the time of the Empire, *that it was still the Church that was in question, whereas contemporary thinkers were, in Europe at least, already debating the essence of religion.* The hierarchy made all the less effort to keep up with the discussion on finding it of trifling importance in view of the political circumstances of 1815–30, which made it possible to restore "Christianity": that is, to take up the reverie where it had been left off. The consequences were all the more sombre inasmuch as, having lost the "élite", the Church did not for long continue in the consolation of keeping the "masses" who were indifferent to these ideological battles and had been driven back upon their own aspirations. It took some time before the Church authorities realized what had happened to the comfortable series of repetitions of an archetype of Christianity that was in defiance of the modern world—as the philosophers of the Enlightenment had postulated.

I. THE TRUE AND THE FALSE CHURCH OF THE ENLIGHTENMENT

It was a well-founded postulate, in terms of the European Church of the eighteenth century modelling its blind tactics on those of the State. In the reign of Louis XV, it would seem that the judicial courts hardly had any other objective than to impede in every way possible the application of the bull *Unigenitus* (1713), and then, from 1750 on, to give themselves up wholly to highly nuanced questions of confession permits and refusals of the sacraments. During a second period (1756–70), the judicial courts revolted against the authoritarian monarchy and fed their political and fiscal grievances with theological arguments dear to the hearts of the third-generation Gallicans and Jansenists.[5] These, particularly, entered into atypical alliances with their erstwhile enemies and became, towards 1770, the mainspring of a sacred union, which was joined, in their turn, by the sympathizers of the movement in Spain, Portugal, Italy and the Low Countries. With a mixture of quite different motives and interests, this sacred union of a few "philosophers", lawyers and churchmen put immense effort into achieving their goal—the overthrow of the Jesuits. It would be more exact to say, with the Liberals of the nineteenth century, that they were trying to deal not so much with the Society of Jesus as the "Jesuit phenomenon" that it stood for. A vast number of publications throughout the world had for a long time attacked the various aspects of this phenomenon; religious Jesuitism had been denounced since the *Lettres Provinciales* of Pascal, mainly for its morals, grown lax on account of probabilism; it gave rise to an economic Jesuitism based on usury and even the extortion of funds, for which it was denounced in regard to the two-million francs crash of P. de Lavalette, the ecclesiastical bankrupt, Visitor General of the Society, and Apostolic Prefect. His trial before the Paris judicial court in 1761 attracted a crowd of malcontents and especially his Dutch creditors. Hack journalists with a sense of the opportune profited from the occasion to remind their readers that the Jesuits were the cruel persecutors of the Church of Utrecht, which was nevertheless valiantly defended by the Doctors of Louvain and the Sorbonne, and by a number of Spanish bishops whom Rome wanted brought before the Inquisition. Charles III of Spain, exasperated by the Madrid and Barcelona disturbances of 1766, instigated—so it was said—by the Jesuits, called together a commission of five bishops to ask their advice. The president, the Archbishop of Burgos, plainly declared in November 1769 that the persecution "of the Church of Utrecht by the Jesuits, who use no weapons other than satire, lies and imposture, has certainly been the cause of the attack made in this regard on the religion of the popes". This was a characteristic condemnation; it was a question of undermining the natural supports of the Society: the papacy and the monarchs. On this last point—political Jesuitism—it was sufficient

[5] J. Egret, *Louis XV et l'opposition parlementaire* (Paris, 1970).

to show that the theology of the Jesuits supported the thesis of regicide. In 1729, a military historian, the Chevalier de Folard, had accused the Society of a plot to gain control of Europe by overthrowing the kings. By an extraordinary transmutation, the argument of his book passed whole and entire into the curious treatise of the Eudist Lefranc, murdered at the Paris Carmelites' house in 1792. His *A Veil lifted for the Edification of the Curious, or the Secrets of the Revolution revealed with the aid of Freemasonry*, attributed to the Masonic plot the misdeeds of the Jesuit plot. There was a supplementary note because of the hardening of the Catholic élite with the dawn of the Revolution: Freemasonry was becoming the "quintessence of all the heresies which divided Germany in the sixteenth century". This, of course, referred to the Protestants and "all those who attack the mysteries of the revealed Religion".[6]

Twenty years after the dissolution of the Society of Jesus by Clement XIV (1773), heresy was still being branded without a realization that this criterion of "Christianity" had undergone a transition from the dogmatic to the socio-cultural level, even when the champions of the Counter-Reformation were propagating a new style of civilization among their colleges, the intellectual and artistic élites, and the governors and missions overseas.

From the seventeenth to the eighteenth century, not only the errant believer became a heretic but the group of opponents who were capable of affirming another set of cultural certainties, and who were daring enough to contest the structures of the society in which the Church had enmeshed itself. Under these conditions, it became very difficult to decide whether the "heretic" of the Enlightenment, in quest of the true Church, was not in fact initiating a civilizing process.

It would seem at first that the Scholastic universe which supported the Ultramontane Church must necessarily have collapsed with the disappearance of the Jesuits, and that the Aristotelian-Thomist understanding of man ought to have given way to the Augustinian vision propounded by the modernist victors after

[6] M. Defourneaux, "Complot maçonnique et complot jésuitique", *Ann. Hist. Révol. Française*, 180 (1965), pp. 170–86.

1770. But this was not the case, for the mental reactions remained the same, as if the ecclesiastical groups were incapable of acquiring a new consciousness. How did the archetype of Christianity manage to survive under the onslaught of its critics? One must certainly refer here to the end of the sacred union on the morrow of the victory over the Society of Jesus: the *Parlementaires* abandoned the balance of religious forces for the direct political struggle against the absolutism of the monarchy; the Tridentines who were anxious about Gallican liberties hesitated between their loyalty to Rome and a frank gesture towards the Enlightenment; as for the Jansenists, their behaviour expressed a malaise common to all the ecclesiastical groups. Their leaders, the lay canon lawyers Maultrot and Camus, a future deputy to the National Assembly, and the Abbé Jabineau, supported the parish priests' accusations of "episcopal despotism" —mainly in the dioceses of Lisieux and Auxerre. But, after 1784, there was a fracture not only in regard to the aims of the party, but to a socio-cultural option.[7] Like many Gallicans, some Jansenists were worried both by the rise of philosophic disbelief and the popular ferment. The years 1784–87 were marked by a doctrinal hardening, as is shown by the Jansenist periodical *Nouvelles Ecclésiastiques*. It put forward a kind of "cultural aristocratism", the product of a retreat from criticisms that it had been the first to formulate. This was the time when Beaumarchais and Restif de la Bretonne were alarmed by the "disquieting faces that looked out of the Paris nights". In Christian circles, a new sacred union was about to form once again on the eve of the Revolution, no longer so much as a common front against the Ultramontane system, but as a rampart of Christianity in the face of the social subversion imputed to the spread of the Encyclopedists' theses. Once again, the necessity of maintaining a Christian civilization took precedence over the ecclesiological quest.

A major movement disputed the validity of this deviation, the

[7] E. Preclin, *Les jansénistes du XVIIIe siècle et la Constitution civile du clergé* (Paris, 1929), pp. 318, 324–8, 339. B. Plongeron, "Une image de l'Eglise d'après les Nouvelles Ecclésiastiques (1728–1790)", *Rev. Hist. Egl. de France*, 151 (1967), pp. 241–68.

supporters of the Catholic *Aufklärung* (Enlightenment):[8] Grégoire in France, Scipion de Ricci in Italy and Climent in Spain, looked to the universities for support in their attempt to realize the gospel message by means of the natural values of the Enlightenment; for instance, the return to Nature would, it was argued, renew a spirituality of simplicity and poverty (the struggle against episcopal ostentation, holydays of obligation, and so on...). But were their theses, as summarized at the Synod of Pistoia (1786), free of "suspicion" of the pontifical monarchy?[9]

In the course of the Revolution, they would normally have led to the development of a new schema of the Church, centring wholly upon collegiality (the French national councils of 1797 and 1801), and supporting the new philosophy of the Christian-and-citizen. But the French constitutionalists and Italian Jansenists were manifestly at odds when it was a question of putting into practice above all the freedom of religious cults written into the constitution of year III of the Revolution. These apostles of pluralism were not resigned to the abandonment of a mentality centred upon "Christianity", and still fought for a Catholic Church of the majority recognized as such in the State. "Secularization" was a transient evil which had to be tolerated; they refused to consider theology in the same way, but dispensed a penitential morality adapted to a *"Christianitas afflicta"*—a theme dear to the Ultramontanes grouped around the persecuted Roman centre.[10] Napoleon knew how to reap the harvest of an unexpected consensus of the rival groups. He nullified the ecclesiological quest of the preceding years and favoured the juridical bent of a Church which he reassured by including it in his establishment. The Imperial Church already bore witness to the key terms of the Restoration: *Order* and *Repose.*

[8] B. Plongeron, "L'Aufklärung catholique en Europe occidentale (1770–1830)", *Rev. Hist. Mod. et contemporaine*, XVI (1969), pp. 555–605. "Questions pour l'Aufklärung catholique en Italie", *Il Pensiero Politico*, III (1970), pp. 30–58.

[9] C. A. Bolton, *Church Reform in 18th century Italy. The Synod of Pistoia* (The Hague, 1969).

[10] B. Plongeron, *Conscience religieuse en Révolution* (Paris, 1969), pp. 171, 177, 199, 211. "Problèmes de Théologie politique sous les IIe Lumières", *Acte du 3e Congrès Intern. des Lumières* (Nancy, 1970).

II. TRUE AND FALSE RELIGION (1795–1815)

From the devotion to the Sacred Heart, the ultimate achievement of the Christocentrism of the seventeenth century, to the theory of religious emotion represented by Schleiermacher's *Discourse on Religion*, by way of Rousseau's *Profession du foi du Vicaire Savoyard*, there was a clear degeneration of the notion of a "religion of the heart". Its effect on the last representatives of the Enlightenment was all the more indelible inasmuch as the Christian people eager for mysticism and miracles (in this eighteenth century that is so wrongly thought to have been rationalist) were able to satisfy themselves by means of aberrant and subterranean forms of the kind which led the Jansenist "convulsionaries" of Saint Médard to enthuse over the prophetesses of the Revolution, Suzanne Labrousse and Catherine Théot. What did the Church have to offer when the torment was over?—The aesthetic apologetics of the *Génie du Christianisme* and the cry of its author, Chateaubriand: "I have wept and I have believed." This was in alignment with the direction of the German Romantics, and dangerously emphasized the immanentism which caused the Catholic Church willingly to celebrate happy ignorance, the support of the faith of humble people.

Did this make Catholicism more attractive? It was hardly Catholicism which drew the many travellers from across the Rhine, among whom was Benjamin Constant, possessed by religious fervour. In 1804 he summarized very neatly the reasons for the universal craze: "Every day the Protestant religion in Germany becomes more *a matter of feeling than an institution*: no forms at all, no symbols, nothing obligatory, almost no ceremonies, nothing but comfortable ideas and an ethics of sensibility."[11] This was the basis of the quarrel: the Church might well bring its apologetics up to date, it remained an institution which was sure of itself in the security of its cult; once again, it was reproached for its rigidity, its Scholastic parrotry, because it wanted to be "one and Catholic". This was the essence of the controversy between Schleiermacher and the Tübingen school. Among others, one author who called himself "Catholic, English and Roman", had

[11] Quoted by J. M. Derré, *Lamennais, ses amis, et le mouvement des idées à l'Epoque romantique* (Paris, 1962), p. 75 .

warned, in 1801, of the possible confusion of religion and cult when the Church was re-established as an institution by the Concordat: "It is the cult, they say, which is to be re-established, and not religion." Was this a specious distinction? "The teaching of the truth of dogmas, of morals, of the duties of religion; the catechism which teaches them, the preaching which confirms them; are these the attributes of the cult? This ultimate seal of Christianity and its ultimate; its precepts which emanate from the one, and its means for arriving at the other: do these comprise *religion*, or do they merely constitute the *cult*?"[12]

In default of a reply, the inhibition of religion by the cult led to a dual process: anticlericalism and indifferentism. Whether it was the product of Gallican ideas, or of the Left and therefore of a more political tendency, anticlericalism was propounded in the context of liberalism, the movement of progress and enlightenment. Many liberals repudiated the apparent antinomy of liberalism and Christianity; some went further and asserted, together with Mahul, a Deputy in 1822, that "liberal ideas are only the development and application of the principles of the Gospel to the government of societies". The principles of the Gospel referred to a "pure Christianity" which contradicted the "Roman cult", an object of as much curiosity as annoyance on the part of the American Protestants visiting France. The liberal Paganel supplied the reason: "Recently some philosophers have been content to regard as problematical the possibility of reconciling the freedom of a great nation with the exclusive profession of the Roman cult; others have resolved the problem negatively, arguing from the inflexibility of the dogmas and axioms on which the immovable policy of the rulers of the Church rests. . . . The unity of the Catholic cult is a fundamental law; but its external accessories are by and large the products of time, of fantastic superstitions, or even of ceremonies taken from paganism with any analogy or any connection with pure Christianity."[13]

The criticism of the cult was directed not only at the Catholic

[12] *Courrier de Londrès*, vol. 50, Third letter of 30 September 1801.
[13] G. de Bertier de Sauvigny, "La vie catholique en France sous la monarchie constitutionelle, vue par les voyageurs américains", *Rev. Hist. Egl. de France*, LV (1969), pp. 243–77. G. Paganel, *De l'Espagne et de la liberté* (Paris, 1820), pp. 35–7.

ministers, but at the Church as an institution, inasmuch as the cultic ceremonies crystallized a "time" which was alien and hostile to liberal "time".

In this way, the actual social influence of the Catholic religion was put in question. It was a problem opened up under the Enlightenment (with a great deal of fuss) by Dupuis and his *De l'origine de tous les cultes* (1796). The significant sub-title "On Universal Religion" called for scientific criticism of the essence of religion.

Egyptology and the discovery of the zodiacs, which were to confound Mosaic chronology and the authenticity of the Pentateuch, undertook the task. These were debates which excited the scholars of Europe who were already enthused by the beginnings of the comparative history of religious systems. The conclusion which they all underwrote was reacted to by the Catholic Church only with an obsolete apologetics and a furious anathema. It remained satisfied with the syllogism repeated later by Deschamps: "The true Church is that described in the Scriptures; but the Church described in the Scriptures is evidently the Catholic Church; therefore...". Why, under these conditions, did the Catholic Church interrupt its monologue to meddle in exegetical research into the authenticity of the Scriptures when the philosophers, smarting under the revival of neo-Platonism after 1815, declared that God could not be the direct object of a direct power of cognition? Certainly they allowed that in default of knowing God in Jesus Christ, it was possible to apprehend the "manifestation" of the Deity. This "manifestation", the Catholics retorted, is none other than the Church which shows itself to be credible by virtue of the cultic signs which are the object of its faith. Certainly the founders of neo-Christianity were straining their ingenuity to overcome the misunderstanding.

III. TOWARDS A SYNTHESIS OF CHURCH AND RELIGION: THE
CHRISTIANITY OF THE RESTORATION (1815–1830)

Does this mean that these founders were confounded by an aggressive anachronism? To the extent to which their designs were inspired by a counter-revolutionary desire to restore the society and the politics of the *Ancien Régime*, this is true. But an analysis which set out to show the concept and the value of time as held by all the champions ôf the idea of post-revolutionary Christianity would reveal more dynamic elements in their repetitions of the archetype. The success of the "theoreticians of divine right" resulted primarily from profound agreement with the sensibility of the time, to the extent to which they extolled a unity of thought which broke a critical and individualistic Enlightenment spirit overprinted by Protestantism. By connecting, like Bonald, society, religion and politics, they shared in the thirst for ecumenism of the societies that had been shaken by revolutionary upheaval: a thirst for the one same way of feeling, thinking, loving and living.

It was a visionary form of the same aspiration which fed the romantic Christianity of Novalis. In his *Christianity or Europe* (1799), he idealized the "splendid times" when Europe was Christian. He rejected Protestantism, the instigator of division, and even attacked Luther. He detected in France and in Germany the symptoms of a religious resurrection, and hoped for a return to unity; he dreamed of the regeneration of Europe and perpetual peace between states. This intuition was precisely echoed by an atheist and anti-Romantic liberal, Saint-Simon, who published his Carolingian dream in 1814: *On the Reorganization of European Society*—a dream of a new Golden Age of Germany and Europe.

Nevertheless this was a unanimism to which some religious ideologues in France were opposed. Joseph de Maistre, in his *Considérations sur la France* (1796), expressed his fear of a *type* of man being propagated as if it actually existed. Certainly the world contained French, English, Italian men, and so on, but the more or less *abstract man* of the *Social Contract* was only a dangerous fiction. At the level of this social immanence, the Liberals recognized their favourite themes in the schema developed by the traditionalist French press: from the *Conservateur* (founded by Chateaubriand in October 1818, together with Bonald, Lamennais and Genoude) to the *Mémorial catholique* (January 1824). The schema comprised an exaltation of the rural family, preserved from revolutionary destruction and the dangers of urban evils symbolized by the "dangerous classes": the workers and layabouts, sowers of immorality. The rural family continued to respect the social hierarchy in the person of the father, the archetype of the family, religion and society.[14]

The receptacle of the threefold theory of familial, royal and divine paternalism became the Church, the benefactor of society, and therefore the controller of the destiny (i.e., the salvation) of Christians. The Restoration catechisms insisted on this main theme as much as on the duty of attaining to salvation in the social state to which one had been called.[15]

It was here, in the sense of this article, that the model (pattern) of Catholicity encountered the same basic problem posed by the Enlightenment: If salvation is an individual affair, as the catechisms after 1820 restated it, how can the Church call itself "catholic"? How can it promise social happiness to men who are excluded from sharing in Christianity by the adage which was more alive than ever: *No salvation outside the Church*?

The defenders of Catholicity of the years 1820-30 could give no answer by reason of a contradiction between their social immanentism and their religious transcendentalism. They divided what they sought to unite, and took refuge in a "Christian time" which was particularly dangerous for the social credibility of the Church. In his *Essay on Indifference* (1817-23), the Ultramontane Lamennais defended the "universal reason", the source of the "common sense", to which all individual reason is subordinated. Bonald echoed the sentiment in his philosophic testament, *Political Meditations drawn from the Gospel* (1830): "In comparing in this (political and social) regard the idolatrous world, the pagan world, the Mahometan world, the non-savage world and the philosophic world, as produced by the Revolution, with the Christian world, I have been brought to *believe* that the truth is in Christianity, and that it has always been there." Therefore it was by an *a priori* that one had to confess that man was contained in the family, the family in the State, the State in religion, religion in the Universe, and the Universe in the Immensity of God; that history was the realization in time of the intentions of God; and that the Pope was their repository: so

[14] R. Deniel, *Une image de la famille et de la société sous la Restauration* (Paris, 1965).

[15] E. Germain, *Parler du Salut? Aux origines d'une mentalité religieuse* (Paris, 1967).

that if there were "no longer a pope there would no longer be any sovereignty, and if no sovereignty no unity, and if no unity no authority, and if no authority no faith".[16] The fragility of this pyramidal vision of society and of the Church, enclosed in a "time of Christianity", would seem to have escaped notice. The Europe of the Holy Alliance received with composure the first encyclical (3 May 1824) of Leo XII, who thrashed "tolerantism", "philosophism" and "indifferentism"; and recommended the bishops of the whole world to have recourse to the Holy See "in their travail, doubts and necessities", for "God, according to St Augustine, has located the doctrine of truth in the chair of unity". An excellent opportunity for M. Frayssinous, Charles X's Minister, to extol in the Chamber of Deputies in 1826 those happy times "in which the Church pronounced with sovereign authority not only on matters of faith, but on rules and manners, in which it made laws regarding discipline . . . established pastors and ministers at the various levels of its hierarchy, and unmade them; and corrected the faithful and rejected from the fold its corrupt members".

The crowning touch would seem to have been the revival of the Society of Jesus in 1814 as the agent to realize this closed system. The anti-Jesuitism of the nineteenth century served as a catalyst, and a much more effective one than in 1762, for all forms of social ferment. The spectre of the "Congregation" was not simply a stroke of luck for writers; it became the pretext for a serious confusion denounced by the Gallican Montlosier, between "religion", "congregation" and "monarchy". "This system which arose from the great principle *gladium gladio copulemus* appeared sublime, but I do not think that there is anything more disgusting to all men, and above all the French people."[17]

Truly, the revolt was imminent. When it burst forth in 1830, it revealed two things: the contradiction of a dynamism in the Church and the affirmation of eschatology. Since 1770, the

---

[16] J. de Maistre, *Du Pape* (1819), p. 22. "Lettre à une dame russe sur la nature et les effects du schisme et sur l'unité catholique" (St Petersburg, February 1810).

[17] *Mémoire à consulter sur un système religieux et politique*, pp. 205, 211; quoted according to R. Casanova, *Montlosier et le Parti prêtre* (Paris, 1970).

Church had not ceased to become introverted in regard to a world whose metaphysical crisis it was hardly aware of. But, recalling Voltaire's remark that "God gave raw matter a centrifugal force", it addressed itself to the post-revolutionary world as if to raw matter; that is, it denied the changes which had taken place since 1789. Paradoxically, it was the world which brought the Church to eschatology by virtue of the messianic forces liberated during the 1830 experiment: intellectual, socializing or essentially spiritual messianic currents which introduced a new kind of duration: after the artificially sustained time of "Christianity", there came that of the "barbarians", soon to be extolled by Ozanam. The religious consciousness whose gropings, convulsions and appearances were symbolically embodied in Lamennais was torn between these two modes of "time".

Translated by John Griffiths

Giacomo Martina

The Contribution of Liberalism and Socialism to a Better Self-conception of the Church*

IN his *The Origin, Forms and Development of Religion*, Benjamin Constant asserted that every organized religion tended to become an instrument for conferring privileges on a priestly caste. The same tendency can be seen in many ideologies, especially in politics; many revolutions that started out in the name of justice have ended in the establishment of a new, privileged ruling class. The Catholic Church has not always been wholly free from such a tendency. In the age of absolutism it took its stand on existing rights in its relations with higher authorities; or, in simpler and more familiar terms, if the Church did not accept certain privileges as an historical right, it appeared to be associated with the advantaged rather than the disadvantaged. There were material privileges derived from various ecclesiastical immunities, and local and personal rights, of a varied and complex historical origin, claimed by theologians who supported their arguments by various theories and agreements, with various degrees of emphasis. In these theories, rights appertaining to the Church were said to derive from its very nature; they were defended by the hierarchy against the modern State with a vigour that absorbed a considerable part of their time and energy, and those of the Roman Curia. In concordats concluded in modern times (for example, with Spain in 1737, with Sardinia in 1741, and with Naples in 1742) the defence of immunities takes up

* For a more detailed discussion of the ideas put forward in this essay, cf. G. Martina's *La Chiesa nell'età del l'assolutismo, del liberalismo, del totalitarismo* (Brescia, 1970).

about half the text and displays a casuistry in which, today at least, it is hard to see a genuine concern with religion. Even if one admits (as did the deputy Boncompagni in a debate in the Sub-Alpine, or Piedmontese, Parliament in 1850, on the abolition of the special ecclesiastical courts) that in a society founded on privilege it was difficult to deny the Church privileges which, initially at least, were aimed at defending religious ends; but even if this is conceded, it is impossible to overlook the considerations which Antonio Rosmini advanced in *The Five Wounds of the Church* (written 1832–1833, and published in 1848): "The priesthood, segregated from the people, at a level of ambition, one might say, because inaccessible, was harmful because ambition degenerated into a patrician status, into a unique sort of society separated from all the rest, with its own peculiar interests, laws and customs."

The progress made in clarifying the nature and duties of the modern State, the struggle against privilege which (according to the well-known thesis put forward by De Tocqueville) the absolutist State bequeathed to the liberal State, the assertion of the principle of equality in the eighteenth and nineteenth centuries, announced the death of immunities which were swept away by revolution, or gradually abandoned after a series of diplomatic and legal struggles in which the Church was initially the loser in Latin America and Europe. The loss of immunities, and above all of the special ecclesiastical courts, was deeply regretted by the bishops, afraid of losing their authority over the clergy if they no longer had extra-spiritual suasions. The hierarchy also feared that the clergy would lose respect if put on the same level as the laity— a change which would influence the mind of the Church, and gradually bring about the loss of privilege. Today, without going so far as the deputies who, in 1850, wanted not only to abolish ecclesiastical courts but to deprive the Church of all juridical powers, one can without much difficulty accept many of their arguments, and recognize the justice of the prologue to the law of 30 September 1784, by which Peter Leopold of Tuscany abolished the ecclesiastical courts. The old theories of immunities, still theoretically included in the Code of Canon Law but now fallen into disuse, require a complete re-examination which would bring out their historical validity and show how this was conditioned by times and circumstances. The Church now presents itself not so much as possessing rights but as ready to serve.

This new idea of authority and the priesthood becomes clear on examining the two contrary conceptions of the Church, one characteristic of the *ancien régime*, and expressed in Bellarmine's definition; the other of our age, put forward in radical terms by liberals of different classes, and accepted by Rosmini in his *Five Wounds*. The first conception diminishes to a considerable extent the specific differences between political and ecclesiastical societies; the second lays emphasis on the differences between them. In his definition Bellarmine (which, if not the only one held by the Church, made the deepest impression on the post-Tridentine ecclesiastical mentality) conceives the visible Church as a political power, and compares it with the two States in which dictatorship is strongest and best organized. This was the basis of the desire to safeguard authority through outward display; it conceives the Church as a pyramid in which, just as the State is summed up in the sovereign, so the Church is to be summed up in the Pope, that is, pastoral work is to be carried on with coercive methods. In the nineteenth century, many liberals reduced religion to an exclusive individual and spiritual relationship with God, directed entirely to future life and denying the Church any social function, right of compulsion, and support from the State. After a long sifting of these arguments by Rosmini, Montalembert, Lacordaire, Lamennais, Möhler, Acton and others, the truth (mingled with some error) eventually impressed itself on the Christian consciousness. Rosmini deplored the inadequacy of a policy which aimed at correcting evils "by laws and penalties, by legal means more fitting for temporal regimes than ecclesiastical". He stressed the spiritual and mystical nature of the Church. In this way, the traditional visual conception of the Church was reversed; poverty would become the most efficacious method by which to re-establish the Church's authority; it was an organic conception of the Church, "in which all the faithful, clergy and people, represent and give form to that wonderful unity of which Christ himself spoke" (Rosmini). Hence the suppression of the post-Tridentine clericalism and ecclesiasticism in which the laity (juridically at any rate) had no part to play in the life of the

Church; in which reliance was placed on measures of compulsion; in which there was distrust of aid given by the State, which exacted a heavy price for its support, and deprived the Church of its liberty, most of all in the selection of bishops, combining political and religious opposition to a perilous degree.

This fresh view showed itself most fruitfully in different spheres. Slowly, not without a certain nostalgia, and often more under the pressure of events than through an intimate and spontaneous conviction, pastoral activities changed: they came to be based not on compulsion but on the intrinsic efficacy of the power of truth; in other words, the Church sought to gain the free adherence of the human person, the only form consistent with his dignity. In 1848, the Piedmontese bishops considered that the end of civil sanctions for ecclesiastical censure would mean the collapse of religion; the Tuscan bishops after 1850 were convinced that their denunciation of immorality in the Press was useless if it was not followed up by civil confiscations. But in time the new situation was accepted; the clergy were convinced that to remove dangers to the faithful through official Christian institutions it was better to give Catholic consciences a thorough training.

The fulfilment of "Easter duties" was strictly controlled throughout the *ancien régime* and in Rome until 1870; this was done by an inspection of "Easter certificates" and a series of measures against those who did not conform, going as far as interdict and excommunication. All this came to an end and now the ecclesiastical authorities are content to wait, patiently and confidently, for the free decision of the faithful. The secularization of the States of the Church, which resulted in the end of the Temporal Power, the transfer of religious charities to lay control, the exclusion of the Holy See from international political congresses, and a tendency to emphasize the autonomy of temporal concerns, have freed the bishops and the Roman Curia from innumerable material questions, which took up much of their time and lowered their prestige. All this has recalled the Church to its mission of salvation, purified it, and revealed its true image; and given back to the laity its proper tasks. In other ways the Church became more aware of its rights, and more firmly demanded independence in its relations with the State. Under the *ancien régime*, the Roman Curia was concerned more with the defence of its immunities than with its freedom to make appointments to benefices, large and small. In 1831, in *L'Avenir*, Lamennais raised the cry: "Catholics, we must save our faith, and we shall do this in freedom, our rights. . . . The State should have nothing to do with the selection of bishops and clergy."

But what if freedom led to a denunciation of the Concordat and the loss of State subsidies? Better poverty than slavery! was the reply. This attitude (which the Roman Curia regarded with considerable apprehension, since they felt they could not rely on the heroism of a good part of the French clergy and faithful) was nevertheless maintained, and became widespread in 1848, extending even to the bishops. It met with broad agreement, and in Italy the same idea was spread by Rosmini with a wealth of scholarship and a deep sense of loyalty to the Church. In 1905 it was forced on the Church in France, when it lost its means of subsistence and its property, but instead obtained, for the first time since 1516, freedom to choose its bishops directly, without any intervention by the government.

At first freedom was looked on with marked distrust; it was admitted at the most as a mere administrative procedure, experimentally. But later it came to be recognized solemnly for its intrinsic value, as giving expression to dignity of man in his individual and social condition. Not only was religious liberty solemnly recognized as an essential element of the act of faith, but the rights of public opinion were upheld within the Church itself. In the last resort, this was based on the different charismata conferred on all the people of God as jointly responsible for active work in the life of the Church. The proud and pharisaical sense of "possessing the whole truth" gave place to a recognition of what was "true and sacred" in other religions, or even in many defensive arguments with atheists. The process went so far as to redefine completely the expression *extra Ecclesiam nulla salus*; at the same time emphasis was laid on the Church as an institution in history, continually renewed through the experience of centuries, but never arriving at perfection on earth. Perhaps the various aspects mentioned above may be reduced to one central point: namely, that liberalism has spread, and been accepted first by the Catholic laity, then by the hierarchy, convinced that the freedom of the Church today can be secured not by claiming for it a special juridical regime, but by placing it in the context of freedom in general; that is, by rejecting the *thesis* and accepting the *hypothesis*. In 1830, Archbishop De Méan of Malines made a declaration to this effect in a letter to Congress; Dupanloup repeated it with emphasis in 1848. Montalembert re-affirmed it even more strongly in 1863. Since then, Catholics from all nations have continued to repeat it—from Cardinal Gibbons to anti-Fascists like De Gasperi. It has been the *ktema es sei* which the Church has taken over from liberalism; little by little, liberal society has shown a parallel evolution, with a gradual recognition of religious values.

It may be too easy to establish the influence liberalism has exerted on Catholicism. But it is less easy to describe the contribution made by Marxism and the two political systems it has inspired (Socialism and Communism) to the re-discovery by the Church of its true character. This is not because the assertions of Marxist philosophy first of all, and then of the Communist revolution, did not coincide with a profound re-thinking of Catholics about the nature of the Church, but because the question is still undecided, whether a nexus of cause and effect can be established between the two phenomena, or whether the evolution of ecclesiology does not result from other factors—mainly the new general conditions of society in the twentieth century. We should not forget that for a long time Catholic thinking was dominated by Pius XII's image (an image founded on the material conditions of his time) of an intrinsically evil Communism. It was only later, in Pope John's encyclical *Pacem in Terris*, that a distinction was made between economic doctrines and philosophical arguments. In any case, whether it was the outcome of Marxism or the Industrial Revolution, or not, the conscience of the clergy from the end of the nineteenth century developed in three main directions. The rise of an industrial proletariat sharpened the Church's sense of its own responsibility in the face of poverty. Poverty, of course, has existed in society in all ages, but one might say that today it has been institutionalized by liberal capitalism, and has provoked a real awareness of the problem. The Church did not wait until the twentieth century to concern itself with the care of the poor, but its action was not altogether free from a certain paternalism which is understandable in the light of history but was always associated with a system of privilege; for example, a wealthy hierarchy and laity, with vast landed possessions, gave support to many social enterprises. The same factors were found in nineteenth-century liberalism in the countries of Latin America and Europe. But they were not enough to lead the Church to discover the original features of poverty observed both in individuals and in the collective. Hence a sharper protest was made against an injustice which deprived the Church of some of its intrinsic rights and of the means it required to carry on its traditional work of helping the poor, which had come about as an extension of divine charity towards mankind. We recall many legal steps taken to safeguard some part of the Church's patrimony, certain pious deceptions, and the slow and silent repossession of properties that had been lost. Only in the last few decades, beginning with the end of the First World War, do we become aware of a new outlook. Poverty came to be regarded not only as an evil to be alleviated by means of the superfluous riches derived from the capitalist system but as a value to be secured, as a necessary condition of freedom in relations with the civil authorities and the effective holders of power (high finance) —as the sole effective witness of a new incarnation. Henceforward it was not enough to help the poor unless one shared their lot so far as was possible. The problem of poverty in all its material aspects involved complex questions of law, a revision of the system of social benefits, the renunciation of "stole fees", an end to inequalities among the various ecclesiastical regions, the discovery of new methods of subsistence, up to the institution of the "worker-priests", conceived as witness and not just a means of apostolate; all this was envisaged in a new outlook (cf. *Lumen Gentium*, par. 8, *Perfectae caritatis*, par. 13). It may be asked if this new spirit, the vision of a "Church of the Poor" (*Ecclesia pauperum*), is not a response to the class-solidarity which is undoubtedly one of the main attractions of Marxism. It is not enough, as Congar pointed out in his essay (*Vraie et Fausse Réforme de l'Eglise*, Paris, 1950, pp. 604–22) that Catholics should have an inborn love and respect for order rather than justice. For some decades after the Industrial Revolution and Marx's *Communist Manifesto*, people continued to take as their ideal society one organized on strictly hierarchical lines, in which everyone would from birth have assigned to him his position and occupation; this tended to leave the mass of the people in a state of underdevelopment, not only economically but culturally. Mgr Spalding, Archbishop of Baltimore, once considered the emancipation of American Negroes, brought about by Lincoln, to be atrocious. The provincial synod of Spoleto in 1849, initiating ideas which were to make up the Syllabus of Modern Errors, together with Pius IX listed the most widespread errors as indifferentism, the trend to anarchism and the denial of the right to property. In 1863 the same Pope wrote to Prince Maximilian of Habsburg: "The supporters of revolution everywhere always agree on one thing: to make war on private property and the Catholic Church."

The political, social and economic demands from wide circles of public opinion, which often mixed positive with negative features, were summed up by a majority of Catholics in one proposition: "The Revolution is Evil Incarnate". The substantial successes achieved by Socialists, who were above all Marxists and in any case anticlerical, compelled Catholics, laity and clergy, to take a fresh look at reality; to break away from the myth of the Revolution and appreciate the complex problems underlying it; to make a distinction between the defence of property and that of the Church, and to identify themselves with those whose situation cried to heaven for vengeance. The Church was dangerously linked with capitalism in many countries, but it gradually rediscovered its role as a defender of justice. This was exemplified in the recognition of the legitimacy of trade unions in Leo XIII's definition in *Rerum Novarum* (par. 36): "Those associations either consisting wholly of workers, or of workers and employers together". This was opposed in vain in 1914 by the *Civiltà Cattolica*, and in 1924 by the textile industrialists of Northern France, who made a series of accusations against Mgr Liénart, Bishop of Lille. The *Civiltà Cattolica* had to retract, and Mgr Liénart was made a Cardinal. The foundation of a Catholic trade union movement showed that the Church was making a brave attempt to adapt to new demands; it meant the introduction of Christian values into the social structure of the time, the acceptance of the truths in Marxism and of the legitimacy of resistance in defence of the rights of the oppressed. The Church was not solely, nor even for the greater part, a preacher of submission; it became the guide and inspirer of humanity, of the depressed classes in their painful effort to reach a higher standard of living, of social justice, relying on their own resources and the strength of their claims. No one today would repeat the declaration of the provincial synod of Cincinnati in 1861, that "the spirit of the Church is characterized by its conservatism".

The Church has opposed liberalism and socialism as leading to a materialism that might endanger the supernatural order. A gradual differentiation made it possible for the Church to accept the valid elements in these political movements, and to put them in a fresh context. At the same time both schools of thought have helped the Church to rediscover and express certain aspects of the Christian message which had been obscured in the course of the centuries. To sum up, the Church today understands more than it did that it must serve mankind—"man himself, whole and entire, body and soul, heart and conscience, mind and will" (Pastoral Constitution of the Second Vatican Council, *Gaudium et Spes: The Church in the Modern World*, par. 3).

Translated by Alec Randall

John Schumacher

The "Third World" and the Self-understanding of the Twentieth-century Church

THE first obstacle for the historian who attempts an analysis of the twentieth-century perspective of the Church's self-understanding resulting from its impressive extension in the Third World is one of complexity—the complexity of the term "Third World", and the complexity of its impact on the Church. If we are to define the Third World as those countries "... still seeking the means to escape from the domination of the great powers and to develop freely...",[1] we find very different types of national churches, distinct in their development.

There are, first, the churches which largely grew out of the century of world-wide missionary expansion preceding World War II, an expansion paralleling, and all too often uncomfortably implicated in, the imperialist expansion of the major Western powers in Asia and Africa. They are young churches, and generally minority groups suspect of being alien to the majority culture of their peoples, of which a non-Christian religion seems to form an integral part. In the second place we find the churches which grew out of the Iberian expansion of the sixteenth century. They are churches with well-established traditions, endowed with a hierarchy since the sixteenth century, but also usually stunted in their development through the failure of the *Patronato-Padroado* system to develop an adequate indigenous clergy. Though majority churches are intimately bound up with the culture of their peoples (at times even to an extent

[1] "Message de quelques évêques du Tiers-monde", *La Documentation Catholique* 64 (1967), 1899.

which makes their more vital elements seek to disentangle the church from a suffocating embrace), they too find themselves threatened with the loss of their identity by their excessive dependence on missionaries from abroad. Finally, there are many of the Eastern churches, no less venerable for the antiquity of their tradition than the churches of the West, but by the minority status they occupy in predominantly Muslim countries, likewise struggling to maintain their identity and develop freely.

Though the coming to maturity of the churches of Asia and Africa created by the nineteenth-century world-mission is the most obvious element of the extension of the Church in the Third World, the churches founded in the sixteenth century as well as the Eastern churches of antiquity may be truly said to have entered into the mainstream of Church life only in the twentieth century, and only then to have been accepted—even imperfectly as yet—as equals among the churches making up the People of God. As we have come to recognize, there are many kinds of imperialism and dependency—not only political, but economic, cultural and religious. The political emancipation which has been so rapid since 1945, has only served to heighten the consciousness of other forms of dependency, and to intensify the search for means to eliminate them. Not least is this true in the life of the national churches as they seek, not independence from the universal Church, but a realization by themselves, and a recognition by others, of their own unique character within the universal Church, as well as full integration within their own national cultures.

The entrance into the full life of the Church of these peoples of the Third World, acutely conscious of their aspirations to national development and self-realization, has had a manifold effect on the whole Church's self-understanding. The principal elements in this new self-understanding due primarily to them would seem to be the following: (1) a realization of the essential pluralism amid unity which belongs to the universal Church; (2) a new attitude towards the values of non-Christian religions and consequently a new concept of the relation of the Church to them; (3) a broader understanding of the role of the Church as a witness to the word of God and its demands on men; (4) a fuller concept of the mission of the Church as embracing not only the ministry of word and sacrament, but active involvement in economic and all human development.

Other elements in the contemporary Church's self-understanding might be mentioned, which, though they had their principal origin in a European or North American milieu, have also to some extent been the fruit of Third World experience: for example, the new understanding of religious freedom, and the altered concept of ecumenical relations among the Christian churches. The contribution of the lived experience of Protestants and Catholics working in the Third World has made its own contribution here, too. But the four elements named above would seem to deserve more extended consideration, as being more clearly specific contributions of the Third World.

At a time when the vast majority of Catholics lived within the geographical boundaries of Europe, even the presence of sizeable minorities in "the missions" did not significantly affect the European character of the Church as a whole, for the mission churches were governed by a European hierarchy, and largely, if not exclusively, staffed with a European-born clergy. In spite of the efforts at accommodation on the part of a few missionaries of vision, the Catholicism implanted and lived among the peoples of the mission lands bore the characteristics of its European origin, and the local churches remained essentially appendages of the Church in Europe, itself increasingly centralized and brought into uniformity in liturgy, law and theology.

It would perhaps be an exaggeration to say that the contemporary recognition of the Church as essentially embracing a legitimate pluralism, not only in the forms of its liturgy and law, but even in its theology and the expression of its faith, has been solely due to the striving of the peoples of the Third World to express more fully their own identity and the uniqueness of their own cultures. But the theologian reflecting on the incarnational nature of the Church could not fail to take account of the variety of peoples which had entered into the Church, bearing cultures and civilizations often just as venerable and of greater antiquity than those of the West. The point had not totally escaped the followers of Matteo Ricci in seventeenth-century China, but a European Church had been unable or unwilling to recognize it at the time.[2] In the twentieth century the conclusion could not be so easily evaded, particularly as the Western political hegemony began to fade and the rising nationalisms of the new nations looked back to their own cultural heritage as the source of national spirit to unify their peoples. Once the step of recognizing that Catholicism might express itself differently in Asia than in Europe had been taken, it became clear that even in those peoples who had shared a common experience of a European culture accompanying the implantation of the Church in their midst (as in the countries formerly subject to the Spanish *Patronato*), the cultural heritage, for example, of the Philippine church was not that of the churches of Hispanic America,[3] nor even was the national character of the Peruvian church the same as that of Argentina.

The conscious recognition by the Church of a legitimate and even necessary pluralism in its life has manifested itself most obviously and most readily in the adaptation of the liturgy since Vatican II. The substitution of the vernacular for Latin in the Roman rite, a development aided by the existence of Eastern vernacular liturgies, was a first tangible step. More recently, and as yet somewhat tentatively, the recognition of diverse expressions of worship proper to a plurality of cultures has been accepted. The impulse behind the creation of national episcopal conferences and the widespread desire for greater room for initiative on their part likewise correspond to the realization of the pluralistic nature of the Church. But the area in which the need for pluralism has been most felt has been that of theology itself. Not only those cultures with ancient and well-developed philosophical and religious traditions of their own demand this pluralism, but other peoples whose ways of thought are less obviously distinct to the superficial Western observer, feel strongly the need for an indigenization of theology among themselves. Though the task has scarcely begun in most cases, the reality of its need (if the Gospel is to be truly made relevant to all men) has become ever more evident.

[2] G. Dunne, *Generation of Giants* (London, 1962).
[3] J. L. Phelan, *The Hispanization of the Philippines* (Madison, Wisconsin, 1959), pp. 72 ff. However Phelan judges the "Philippinization of Catholicism" by a rather narrow theological criterion of orthodoxy.

Intimately related to the encounter of a Western Church with the great non-Christian cultures of the non-Western world, has been the Church's changing attitude towards other religions and its relation to them. The encounter did not, of course, occur for the first time in the twentieth century; Christianity had met Islam in the Middle Ages, but the result had been the Crusades; the missionary expansion of the sixteenth century in turn had seen only the hideous work of the devil in the religions it met. It is true that Ricci and his successors had learned to value the ethical system of Confucianism in the Jesuit mission to seventeenth-century China, and Roberto de Nobili had even perceived some of the religious values of Hinduism. But even apart from the rejection of their views by the European Church, their fundamental attitude was rather one of openness to what might be found compatible with Christianity than a seeking of positive values in the religion of the peoples they were striving to convert. Their understanding of the Church itself was scarcely altered.

The twentieth-century Church, however, has not merely made an effort to understand the religion-inspired cultures with which it lives in contact so as to be able to present its message in their culture-forms. Rather it also looks at them to find true religious values which perhaps have been obscured in the Western Christian presentation or formulation of God's word to man. It even finds in them in some fashion authentic vehicles of God's saving grace in which men truly find him.[4]

This in turn implies an altered concept of the Church itself and its mission to the nations, an understanding which has as yet perhaps not been fully clarified. But whatever the full understanding of the mission of the Church today maybe, few would disagree that an essential part of it is its role as witness to, and servant of, God's word to men—however that may be expressed. To be sure, the Church has always conceived itself as a witness to God's word, and one can certainly not deny all understanding of humble service to Christians of earlier ages. Yet one must confess that the Church's understanding of its witness to God's revelation has

[4] Cf. the decree *Nostra Aetate* of Vatican II, and more explicitly, "Conclusions du Symposium sur la théologie de la mission", sponsored by SEDOS, 27–31 March 1969; in *La Documentation Catholique* 66 (1969), pp. 887–9.

usually been that of the Crusader, the Inquisitor, or—in modern times—the beleaguered and persecuted defender of the truth against modern atheism.

The most striking manifestation of this self-understanding of the Church as witness to and servant of God's word, wherever found, is the one which has been forced on it most clearly by the Third World in its midst. It is the role of the Church as bearing a responsibility for all human development, even for temporal and economic development. For it is precisely the deprivation of economic development, and as a consequence, of access to other forms of national and human development which constitutes the Third World as such. Again, to be sure, the Spanish church which produced Francisco de Vitoria and Bartolomé de las Casas was not totally deaf to the cries for justice in the preaching of the Gospel to developing peoples.[5] But the justice of which the Church recognizes itself as prophet today has another content. It is no longer a question primarily of individual rights but of the rights of nations. Moreover, the presumption in favour of legitimately acquired wealth no longer exists for nations. In the face of the growing gap between the nations which possess and those which do not, and which cannot acquire the means of doing so, the Church sees itself as committed to demand the liberation of the Third World from the forces inherent in an international situation tending to maintain that imbalance of justice.[6]

Yet the prophetic role of the Church in its demand for justice for the Third World does not fully express its conception of itself today. It must also play an active role in the achievement of economic development, and through it, of all human development. The Church must actively involve itself in temporal realities, not to dominate, or to control, but to promote effectively and assist in its servant role the attainment of a human society in which human culture and development are available to all men. Again it can be noted that this is not the first time that the

---

[5] Cf. L. Hanke, *The Spanish Struggle for Justice in the Conquest of America* (Philadelphia, 1949); J. Hoffner, *La ética colonial española del Siglo de Oro* (Madrid, 1957) (*Christentum und Menschenwürde*, Trier, 1947).

[6] *Gaudium et Spes*, no. 86; *Populorum Progressio*, nos. 47–9, etc.

Church has played an active role in the human and even economic development of nations, as both the history of medieval
Europe and the history of "the missions" bear witness. The difference perhaps lies in the view of the work of development not
merely as a means to attract men to the Gospel, nor even as a
kind of pre-evangelization, to establish the necessary human conditions in which the word can be preached. Rather this contribution to human development is increasingly recognized as an
integral part of the mission of the Church, so that even if there
is no possibility of actually preaching the word or administering
the sacraments, the Church, by its contribution to human development, is fulfilling its mission of working for the realization of God's kingdom.[7]

If the history of the Church is a progress in its understanding
of itself, to what extent has the evolution sketched here affected
Catholic ecclesiastical historiography? For the most part, the
judgment must be quite negative. The writing of Church history has increasingly detached itself from the older models in
which popes and emperors, councils and heresies, and the vicis-
situdes of ecclesiastical politics and diplomacy occupied the centre
of the stage. The shift in emphasis in secular historiography from
political and diplomatic history to social, cultural and economic
history, has been paralleled in Church historiography by a shift
of interest to the life of the People of God, their faith and their
spirituality, their forms of piety and even their superstitions—it
is these which the ecclesiastical historian seeks to understand and
depict.

Yet when one looks to the standard manuals of Church history, and even to some multi-volume extended treatments,[8] the
result is disappointing to the Church historian or theologian
working in the Third World.[9] At worst, they are narrowly

[7] Cf. P. Land, "*Populorum Progressio*, Mission, and Development",
International Review of Mission 58 (1969), pp. 400–409.
[8] The two major multi-volume series currently in progress, the *Handbuch der Kirchengeschichte*, edited by H. Jedin, and *The Christian Centuries: A New History of the Catholic Church*, edited by L. Rogier, R.
Aubert, M. D. Knowles and A. G. Weiler, have not yet reached a point in
publication chronologically advanced enough to make possible a judgment
on them with regard to this point.
[9] E. Dussel, "Cultura latinoamericana e Historia de la Iglesia", *Anuario
de Sociología de los Pueblos Ibéricos* 5 (1969), pp. 113–18.

national histories focusing events upon the preoccupations of the national church of the author. At best they are conceived on the broader scale of Europe, with increasing attention being given to the experience and piety of the Eastern churches. But the rest of the Third World (Latin America, South and East Asia, and Africa—if they appear at all) is treated in a few pages. What is worse, these appendixes, besides being limited for the most part to the barest facts of the foundations of these "missions", commonly include numerous errors of fact in the meagre information they supply.

The "mission histories", though filling the gap to a certain extent, and somewhat less inaccurate in their factual presentation, likewise fail to solve the problem. For all churches have been mission churches in their origins. Yet even though no Church historian could conceive ending the history of the German church, for example, with the work of St Boniface, whole Christian peoples numerically larger by far than the German church, disappear from the consideration of the Church historian with the substantial completion of evangelization in the seventeenth century, when their life as churches had scarcely begun. The underlying, though unspoken, theological assumption vitiating such mission histories is that these missions are considered more as manifestations of the Christian life of the church which evangelized them than as new incarnations of the Church in cultures having their own contribution to make to the fullness of the People of God.

If the churches of the Third World, precisely because they are developing churches, have themselves as yet produced little in the way of scientific theological syntheses, each in its own unique fashion has lived and is living the Christian life. A theology which finds a *locus theologicus* in the life of the People of God must consider itself as at best half-true if in practice it leaves out of account the Christian experience of the majority of national or ethnic manifestations of Christian experience—even within the Catholic tradition. But the Christian experience of the Third World churches can only become that *locus theologicus* once it has been brought from the margin into the mainstream of Church history. If the Church historian is to be truly such and not merely an ecclesiastical antiquarian, it is surely far more important to know the progress of Christian life during a single century among one entire people of the Third World than to investigate the *minutiae* of the history of any number of medieval European monasteries, long since extinct.

This much being said, the practical difficulties of such a re-orientation of the historiography of the Church to correspond to its contemporary self-understanding must be confessed. Not only does it require a radical shift of perspective on the part of the Western Church historian to make himself conscious of what we may call the new centre of gravity of the People of God. It also requires an intensive work of research and of self-reflection on the part of the historians of the Third World. For just as the churches of the Third World for the most part have scarcely begun the indigenization of their theology instead of accepting the problematics and formulations of the West, so too they have for the most part done relatively little to write the history of the unfolding of God's grace among themselves. In the urgent pre-occupation with what seemed to be "more necessary" and "more practical" matters, they have failed to lay the foundations for their own particular self-understanding, which alone can be the basis for their perception of their own unique insertion into the history of salvation.

To many today, the task of the Church is to recognize the designs of the Spirit to the extent they manifest themselves in the aspirations of peoples. These aspirations, purified, clarified and energized with the "salt" of the Gospel, help to manifest to the Church its role in each people, its mission to them. The historian of the Church in the Third World must help Christian people to read the signs of the times in their midst, not only in unfolding the history of the People of God in this nation, but in placing it in the context of the whole history of the People of God. Much indeed of what is recounted in the standard histories of the Church has little relevance to the younger churches. But much is very relevant, for it forms an integral part of the continuation of the history of salvation into which the younger churches have been inserted in God's due time. As the Gospel came from Jerusalem through Greece and Rome to Europe, so it has been passed on to most of the Third World through Europe. The task of the Church historian is to delineate what in this past is the particular current into which the history of God's manifestation among this particular Christian people has been inserted. This will be his contribution to the urgent theological enterprise of understanding the Church's mission in this particular people. This in turn will make possible a fuller understanding of itself by the universal Church as the People of God, with all that this implies.

Pierre Delooz

How the Church sees Itself Today

IT WAS not by chance that a sociologist was asked to write the first and last articles in this historical examination of the Church's self-conception. After acknowledging how difficult it is to define the contemporary Church, we may say that it probably sees itself today as part of a whole. No doubt one ought to try to define the special quality of the Church as a part of the whole of human society, to which it is aware of belonging. To ask a sociologist to deal with this question reflects the current desire to analyse as scientifically as possible the way in which the Church sees itself. This desire for a scientific approach is revealing; it shows that the need for scientific objectivity and the attitude of relativization on which this is based are most relevant to the whole question of the Church's self-conception.

Any attempt at a scientific answer will probably be premature because there is insufficient information. Who can say with certainty what a Polish nun, a South American guerilla, a Californian hippie, a Roman prelate or a Coptic fellah living in the Nile valley think about the Church today? All these and many others belong to the Church. In the absence of precise data, we have to some extent to work with hypotheses based on indications which we presume are characteristic.

We lack precise information since it has so far not been possible to interview a representative sample of members of the Church (we do not even know exactly what questions to ask), and in this way to construct a small-scale model of the Church. Therefore we have to concentrate on the most striking aspects of the Church's self-understanding, even though we cannot be at all sure that the less obvious or less easily detected elements are not just as essential. It remains to be seen whether any modern sociologist can provide a framework of facts and ideas to throw light on and define the understanding that an entity as complex as that of the Church can have of itself.

I. FROM IDEOLOGY TO VALUES

The easiest way of dealing with this whole problem would be to draw attention to the various signs of crisis—even of total disruption—apparent everywhere in the Church today. It would be more to the point to try to decide what positive demands have helped to produce these different elements of crisis in the contemporary Church. Often, one image of the Church is destroyed before we are able to define the precise characteristics of a new image, but we can almost always to some extent more surely predict the forces which will herald the future than the damage they may cause.

The unprecedented flow of information now circulating not only throughout the world but within the Church has a powerful impact on the minds of Christians and modifies and changes their ideology. Whatever our status in the Church, the changes in the world force us to ask radical questions about the ideas and doctrines that we hold; and most of us realize that these theories are, at least in part, inadequate. They cannot answer our questions, and cannot even reach the level at which the questioning is taking place. This fact, true of all ideologies, whether religious or not, enables us to understand that the Church's ideology (its doctrinal or theological systems) has become increasingly inadequate because it cannot adapt to the changes in the life of the Church.

On the other hand, Christians are also becoming increasingly aware, on the positive side, of the values by which they live. There is a growing gulf between the Church's doctrinal and theological systems, which seek to justify these values, and the living Christian experience of the values which they feel to be important in their lives. The Church's theoretical systems are proving less and less suited to the task of assimilating contemporary Christian experiences of these values, and tend to become as valueless as any other out-of-date ideology.

In view of this, it would obviously be less useful to try to revive, popularize or modernize one or other of the Church's theologies than to consider the whole problem on the basis of living Christian values. These values will give us the key to the Church's understanding of itself today. If we openly recognize that the Church's theological systems are to some extent discredited nowadays, or that they arouse indifference or even contempt, this does not mean that we are unaware of what is expected from theology. It is clear that the Christian experience of living values in new conditions of life goes together with a desire for a renewed theology which will be open to all these signs of change. On the other hand, it is probably too early for any chance of real success in this sphere. However, what we are witnessing today is an awareness of the need for a new way of interpreting tradition—of seeing this less as something past and more as an experience of the present, so that our task is to decipher what it means for us now. What is taking place in the Church is important enough to merit the closest possible attention. We must be faithful to the past, but we must look forward, and interpret the present accurately.

II. FROM CERTAINTY TO SEEKING

The enormous flow of information reaching the Church from every quarter has resulted in its idea of itself becoming less absolute and more relative. It no longer regards itself as "perfect", but as a "poor servant". It is aware that society as a whole is at present undergoing a test, and that the Church is intimately connected with this experience, which calls it into question and for which it has no ready-made solutions.

This ever-increasing flow of information has also made the Church think more of abandoning its traditional attitude of absolute certainty, and become a seeking Church. There is greater emphasis on the value of the Church's presence in a world, the meaning of which Christians, together with other men, are trying to understand. This attitude in turn implies a greater stress on basic values such as sincerity and authenticity, which are seen not as subjective self-satisfaction, but as a quest for scientific objectivity. This urgent desire for authenticity is visible everywhere in the Church and threatens to overthrow all its traditional and hitherto apparently certain and "unchanging" truths.

Nothing is exempt from this search for authenticity: liturgy, biblical exegesis, speculative theology, ecumenical activity, contacts with non-believers, canon law, and monastic and religious life. Everywhere in the Church, the desire for truthfulness and the need to distinguish what is essential from what is of secondary importance are making themselves felt. Of course there is great resistance to this quest for truth, but, to take one example, the simple annulment of a defensive law of the Church—the Index—shows that this movement is to some extent officially recognized. The Church's attitude towards man's freedom of conscience in the course of a century is also indisputable. In *Mirari vos*, Gregory XVI saw this as a "frenzy resulting from a diseased indifferentism"; and it was, in fact, a weapon turned against the Church at that time. Yet the Second Vatican Council was led to proclaim the legality of freedom of conscience. What the Council undoubtedly had in mind here was primarily man's moral conscience, but it is impossible to recognize the freedom of moral conscience without at the same time recognizing the more general value of the conscience as an attempt to be a presence in the world and indeed to be this world present to itself.

In this changed environment, the Church has come fully to accept both the authenticity of the scientific approach and the limitations imposed on science by scientists themselves—in other words, not to go beyond the relative limits of their affirmations. The validity of science is so widely recognized in the Church today that a bishop could, for example, say at the Second Vatican Council that if there was any conflict between science and faith, it would have to be solved by a process of free scientific research. The Church is certainly not trying to destroy itself in its acceptance of the scientific solution (and similarly in its acceptance of the need to allow a greater exercise of free conscience). On the contrary, its aim in so doing is to make sure that it has the means not only of self-preservation, but for it to do its work in the world to which it is committed.

It is probably too early for us to measure the effect that the sciences have on the Church, but there can be no doubt that the Church's image of itself has already been modified by, for example, biology, psychology (and here especially psychoanalysis) and sociology (in this case, probably indirectly by means of linguistics and social anthropology). This is, of course, no more than a beginning, but the most important effect has probably been that the image that Christians have of the world has been modified by science, and that this inevitably has had repercussions on their image of the Church. Many of the apparently disturbing characteristics in contemporary Christian behaviour certainly have to be explained in the light of this increasing value placed on the human conscience, of this quest for authenticity and desire to be present in the world. There are clearly certain negative characteristics of this need for authenticity—the decrease in the number of vocations for the priesthood and the religious life, the decline in the practice of confession and the widespread reluctance to accept the full implications of *Humanae Vitae*, for example—but, even if its full fruits cannot be seen yet, this need has an undeniably positive value.

III. From Observance of the Law to Creativity

Observance of the law has never been the inflexible practice of the Church. The foundation of new religious orders was forbidden by the Fourth Lateran Council, but dozens were founded one after the other as soon as the Council closed and showed how creative the Church could be. Nowadays, under the pressure of values such as authenticity, with its constant appeal to the human conscience, the really essential and creative value would seem to be freedom. The Church is aware that it must create something new, and that its traditional models cannot embody the values of freedom and of conscience which have come so much to the fore in recent years. The unfortunate distance between the Church's models—in the sense of guides for action—and its values—in the sense of what is experienced as important in life—has certainly led to indifference to, or abandonment of, numerous attempts to create new structures. All the same, there are many promising creative endeavours in the Church. For example, the Church is no longer content simply to make high-sounding declarations of intention, and no longer demands conformity and obedience to the law. It is conscious of what those outside the Church think about it, and seeks justification for what it does in concrete, positive results. It is less rigid and more accommodating, less cautious and more alive—perhaps more so than at any other time. It takes risks in the process of renewal— for example, in the growing dialogue with non-Christians, and in its more active social and political commitment.

All this has, of course, led to less uniformity in the Church, to a greater freedom for the individual to act on his own initiative, to more decentralization, and to an increase in tension and even in conflict; yet all this is the inevitable consequence of a more dynamic expression of creative freedom. There is greater freedom of expression in the spoken and written word. Views can be expressed, and those of others can be contradicted in a free atmosphere of mutual respect. The possibility of failure is freely accepted. These are all signs of creativity, and they make it possible for ordinary believers to see the positive aspect of events which might otherwise be difficult to understand. There are, after all, many otherwise inexplicable happenings in the Church. Bishops adopt apparently contradictory attitudes in public. Many priests leave the priesthood, and this is officially accepted. There are seemingly spontaneous changes in the liturgy. Aspects of faith and morals which have hitherto been inviolable are now openly discussed and disputed. It is not difficult to think of many other examples. We may say that, as a necessary condition of growth, the Church accepts contradiction, conflict and even failure in suffering but at the same time in hope.

IV. From Mere Membership to Responsibility in the Church

The Church is learning (though not without some difficulty) to accept creativity as a positive value, because interpersonal relationships—a loyalty to individual persons rather than to the institution of the Church—are increasingly recognized to be of paramount importance. Purely legal—or sentimental—member-ship of the Church as an institution could—and still can—have its place, but it is rapidly giving way to the current demand for authenticity in a community in which individuals fully accept each other and each other's differences.

Of course no Christian has ever really believed that simply to belong to the Church was enough, but nowadays, understanding itself as it does, the Church clearly aims to be an authentic com-munity of persons who are equal, united, interdependent and responsible for each other and the whole of mankind. This is clearly an ideal which is not always realized, but there are signs that it is being put into practice. Let me give a few examples.

The new idea of marriage and family life in which the wife and the children play a responsible and personal part is becom-ing more and more of a reality. The ecumenical movement, as a responsible human community, is making rapid progress at all levels everywhere. Many of the large religious communities are disbanding and smaller, less strict groups are forming in the conviction that co-responsibility can flourish much better in them. A similar phenomenon is taking place in the Church as a whole, in order to achieve the aim of co-responsibility—an in-creasing decentralization and regionalization at every level. The bishops are meeting more and more in regional conferences, and Christian laymen in small local groups. I think, too, that the in-creasing concern of Christians for world peace on the one hand, and the growing tendency on the part of the "official" Church not to sacrifice living people to abstract principles on the other, are also signs that the ideal of co-responsibility is being realized.

V. FROM SOCIAL INTEGRATION TO SOCIAL OPPOSITION

This growing sense of responsibility for the whole of man-kind has resulted in an increasing awareness in the Church of its social function. In the past, it acted as an agent of social in-tegration, serving to perpetuate the established order and, in extreme cases, to suppress the claims of the people. Now, how-ever, the Church tends more and more to denounce the estab-lishment and to champion the cause of the poor and the op-pressed. As the people of God, it is engaging more and more in political debate and protest on behalf of the poor, acting, in other words, as a social opposition, even if this results in alienation from the establishment.

Contemporary society is marked by often violent opposition between different social groups. Modern man feels isolated from his fellow men even within his social grouping and, if he is materially properous, possessed by the wealth that he thinks he possesses. The quantity of information flowing in his direction is not matched by an improvement in interpersonal communication. The Church, as part of human society, has at last become aware of this situation and is questioning the whole system which has brought it about.

VI. From Religion to Faith

As a consequence of this new understanding of the Church, every Christian has become conscious of the difference between his vocation as a man and as a Christian. The Church is no longer seen as the solution to every human problem—it cannot avert the threat of nuclear war, reduce the distance between the rich and the poor nations, abolish the oppression exercised by bureaucracy, or overcome human alienation. But every Christian knows that he has to accept the challenge presented by these problems and do what he can to make the world more human. The Church is now firmly on man's side, at one with all who are fighting for humanity. But it is also more clearly conscious of its mission. In the last resort, this is not so much to fight for humanity, which is the vocation of all men, Christian and non-Christian, but rather to proclaim the message of Jesus Christ, the message that God loves man as he loves himself.

This, then, is the Church's special task—to reveal God's love for man. This love gives meaning and direction to his life and vocation. The Church has to show him how to be faithful, in his creativity and responsibility, to the demands of his conscience and the claims of freedom in the human community. Above all, however, it has to show him that he can be faithful to his Christian vocation to accept in faith God's love for mankind in Jesus Christ precisely by being faithful to his vocation as a man. This is why the Church appears to dissociate itself more and more from the whole complex of social models which constitutes "religion", without altogether doing away with it.

The emphasis today is not on religion, but on faith as our response to the love God shows for man in Jesus Christ. The Church is allowing "religion" to slip into the background. It is, in other words, becoming "secularized" in order to deepen faith and to stress man's human vocation, as distinct, but not separate from his Christian vocation, so that, through this vocation as man, he may be able to express a Christian vocation that will give meaning and direction to life.

Translated by David Smith

PART II
BULLETINS

Antoine Saucerotte

A Marxist View of the
Self-images of the Church

THE importance of (diachronic) semantics in the future should lead theologians to determine the various denotations and connotations of the word "Church"; for any proficient analysis of the self-conception of the Church must have recourse to modern, structuralist linguistics.

I. THE HERMENEUTIC PROBLEM

Any definition of the Church, not *per se*, but from an heuristic point of view, must take into account the fact that organized Christianity's self-awareness depends wholly on the laws of historic-linguistic change. But then one has to ask whether the Catholic can allow the concept "Church" anything like the fixed, sacred meaning it was alleged—beyond all semantic analysis—to have in the past.

Thomist philosophy would seem to have allowed the Church to have escaped the mutations of historical time by confusing symbol and essence.

But the evolution of modern thought gradually undermined the grandiose conception (still found in Maritain and Gilson, and in—say—Claudel). Ockham and nominalism, then Descartes, identified essence and existence. The impetus had been given to a movement of thought which came to fruition in Marxism where the world was henceforth definitively and totally understood as dominated by the one dimension of historical time. The spirit itself (the ultimate symbol identified by Hegel with an essence distinct from history, though realizing itself through history) vanished, and history appeared henceforth as the only dimension compatible with modern science: the history of men struggling to master matter (Marx); that of an animal species struggling for survival (Darwin); that of the universe of the nebulas and dialectic of Nature.

Henceforth, the Church could no longer lay claim to a God-given essence that placed it outside history. This "exceptional" quality is now seen as relative to the epoch in which it was elaborated, i.e., to the thirteenth century, to the century of Aquinas.

II. THE HISTORICAL PROBLEM

In order to be valid, any heuristic system must accord with the dimension of historical time. When this dimension is universally recognized, the history of the successive self-images of the Church becomes part of the general study of the great superstructures of each period of civilization, and sacred history is seen to be founded on the history of man. History is the history of masses, which act in history only through their group-consciousness: to the extent to which the social group "in itself" becomes a social group "for itself". In these terms, it becomes possible to isolate a number of self-images:

1. The group of the first Nazarene disciples of Jesus developed in the popular Jewish environment of the first century A.D. This environment was marked by an intense religious life, that of the Essenes (living as a community); and that of the Zealots, particularly influential in Galilee (where Jesus lived), who, through their refusal to pay tax, made a stand against Roman domination. To this was added the messianic expectation of the restoration of the Jewish kingdom and full independence. Opposed to them was the Sadducean element of the temple clergy, enriched by offerings and loyal to the Romans, who tolerated the worship of Yahweh (apparently there was no altar to Rome and Augustus at Jerusalem). The moral contestation of the Essenes had, for its part, a sort of philosophy: the Mazdaism which permeated Hebraic gnosticism (e.g., the eternal struggle of the sons of light against the sons of darkness). This conception reappears in

several episodes in the synoptics (when Jesus confronts the Prince of darkness).

Christ's journey to Jerusalem, the acclamations conferring on him the title of "Son of David", the sacking of the temple, then the arrest and the claim, before Pilate, of the title of King of the Jews, and the paying of the penalty, are situated in the above climate.

The first church of Jerusalem grew out of this spirit of contestation, indeed of revolt. It was established through the Ebionites ("the Poor"), through the Montanist revolt which Tertullian supported, and through Donatism and Pelagianism. This tradition upheld poverty, and demanded equality of wealth and the liberation of slaves. It rose up in protest against Roman society as a whole.

2. The self-image of the Pauline churches was very different. They were located in the context of the Hellenistic diaspora, in the Greek cities of Asia Minor, in Greece, at Rome (Epistle to the Romans). Paul was an educated Roman citizen (and a rabbi), and from a well-to-do background. He spent all his youth in a Hellenistic environment (he was from Tarsus). From the time of the conquest and organization of the Roman exploitation of the Orient; from the time of the subsequent immense intermingling of individuals which followed it and entailed the downfall of Roman polytheism, the ground was prepared for the birth of a new religion of salvation which was both individual and universal. This religion (which included Paul as well as slaves) deflected the slaves from a revolutionary struggle against the imperial system in imitation of the Zealot revolts, of the Essene "contestation", and of the revolts in Asia during the time of Pompey, by compensating the humiliation of oppression with the hope of individual salvation after death. In Paul there was an implicit bond between acceptance of the Roman order and the announcement of salvation by Christ. We have left the more or less revolutionary ethics of Jewish messianism to accede to a purely mystical and contemplative level of comprehension. It is well known how a divorce between Paul and the traditionalist party in the church of Jerusalem came about in regard to the observance of Mosaic rites. In fact, the rupture over the rites signalled the advent of a new conception of Christianity, not so

much ethical as mystical, no longer political, but contemplative. This current was enriched with the fourth gospel by the idea of the "Word", which it took from Philo and Greek neo-Platonism. Christ's execution was no longer the condemnation of a Jewish agitator who wished to overturn the Roman order, but became the mystical sacrifice of a son at the behest of the father.

3. It was only in the fifth century that the Church came to think of itself as the essentially sacred symbol. Until then there had been a number of churches: Marcionites, Montanists in Asia, Gnostics at Alexandria, Paulinians at Rome and in Greece. But Constantine's settlement brought about a close association between Christianity and the Empire. The Council of Nicaea, as Constantine wanted, made the Church aware of its unity first by condemning Arius, then by means of the neo-Platonic mystical theology of the Nicene Creed. When the Empire collapsed in the West, the Church to some extent assumed the function of the Roman ruling class. The Empire seemed eternal until, in the fifth century, history forced the Romans to search for the meaning of the swiftly changing events they were living through. The Church, as in *The City of God*, came to see itself in an historical perspective. Augustine did have an intuitive conception of historical time, but one created by God, and running from the creation of the world to its end. In this new dimension the Church became the instrument of divine providence, from its foundation by Christ to the end of time. The symbol became sacred.

But this meant a revival of incipient Mazdaism (taken up by Manichaeus, and even by Augustine). The Church took up the work of battling against Satan and gradually repelling the forces of darkness, by virtue of Christ's gift of the sacramental power of effacing original sin. The Essene baptism, a simple Jewish purification rite, acquired a magical value in association with the Manichaean perspective in which the history of the Church itself was now placed.

4. The strictly historical idea of its own nature which the Church acquired through *The City of God* was appropriate to the problems of the fifth century, when history had become a major human preoccupation.

But, with the Middle Ages, history lost importance. The

strictly eschatological perspective of Augustinianism vanished. From the eleventh century, the Church gradually became identified with the establishment; this was conditioned by the need for the security of a stable, protective feudal hierarchy which might be explained in part by the revival of an agrarian economy. Breaking free from history, like knowledge itself, the Church located itself in the hierarchy of immutable essences which, at the spiritual level, reflected the absolute and definitive feudal order. The Church saw itself as the visible manifestation of the presence of Christ in the world, participating equally in the divine and the human essence. This was how the "Aristotelian-Thomist" Church understood itself, and justified the established order. Thomist philosophy tried to prolong this grandiose, purely synchronic and mythical conception. On the eve of the French Revolution, the Sorbonne was still teaching Scholastic philosophy.

5. But in England, since the thirteenth century, the baronial rebellions had removed the absolutism of the Plantagenets, and —with the usurper, Simon de Montfort—divine right itself. This dealt a severe blow to a Church whose divine essence had been declared immutable. In the first half of the fourteenth century, William of Ockham attacked essentialist philosophy. By identifying essence and existence, nominalism raised for the first time the question of a possible, purely historic nature of the Church; that is, a purely human nature. Ockham was able to triumph at Oxford, and was eventually condemned in Paris, which had become the citadel of Scholasticism.

6. Descartes completed the process when the principles of a rational and scientific knowledge began to emerge. The point of departure of all knowledge could only be in the existence of rational thought. Essentialist philosophy, whose point of departure was located in God the creator of essences, vanished.

The liquidation of the essentialist philosophy by modern thought cut the Church off from its divine "essence" and initiated a new, "humanist" and political understanding of its nature.

In France a new movement of Catholic thought in the seventeenth century took over this new philosophy, which affirmed the inalienable fredom of man. Molina, at the end of the sixteenth century, had cleared the way for the mental attitude of the Jesuit fathers who taught Descartes and, in their college at La Flèche, applauded the discoveries of Galileo. The Oratory joined forces with them when Bérulle urged Descartes to construct the new philosophy. It was only at the beginning of the eighteenth century, when faced with the menace of rationalism, that Rome decided to condemn him.

The Church of the Jesuits regarded itself as an assembly of men responsible for showing the world the greatest glory of God, which is that of Catholic truth; and this political will tended to take the place of the former Providence—though to the detriment of traditional moral theology, which brought on the Jesuits the attacks of the "Provincials". Malebranche clarified the new conception of the relations between man and God. To the latter only "general causes" were reserved. An immense possibility of free action existed for man, where everything else was concerned. The success of Malebranche in the seventeenth century corresponded to a new comprehension which, in France, Oratorians and Jesuits had of the activity of the Church.

But if there was no limit to freedom, there was none to the exercise of reason. Why should man and God, coexistent, restrict themselves? Spinoza resolved the dilemma by putting strictly human reason first, and by confounding God and Nature. Descartes's message was then revealed to be a mortal threat to the civilization of the *ancien régime*, with which the Church was associated. Bossuet had sensed the danger as early as 1670. At the end of the seventeenth century, the crisis in the Catholic Church had become open. Malebranche led to philosophical deism, and this to natural philosophy. These were weapons for the French bourgeoisie rising to attack the *ancien régime*.

7. It was only in the nineteenth century, when confronted by the assault of rationalism, that the Church became aware of itself again as depository of the will of God and guarantor of the order established by him. The "infinite freedom" claimed for man, and the uncontrolled exercise of reason which resulted from it, had finally led to the celebration of reason, incarnated in an actress dancing on the altar of the deconsecrated Notre Dame. At the same time, the sans-culottes questioned even the right to property.

In 1796, in his *Théorie du pouvoir politique et réligieux*, de Bonald showed the need for a return to order, which Napoleon was to follow. In 1800 the Concordat was signed: it was a matter initially of restoring order in the mind. The restoration in 1815 of the Company of Jesus, which had been abolished in 1774 at the demand of the philosophers, reinforced "right-thinking". Now perennial principles had to be reaffirmed. For this, de Bonald said, one had to go back beyond Descartes, and rediscover the divine "essence" of the Church, which would be crowned, as de Maistre urged, by a return to papal supremacy, making the pope, in the terrestrial order, once again guarantor of the celestial God. Ultramontanism expressed this intention. On the morrow of the events of 1830 and 1831, which had witnessed, with the triumph in France of the liberal ideas of the Revolution, the awakening of anticlericalism and the sacking of the Archbishop's palace in Paris, Gregory XVI, in his encyclical *Mirari vos*, condemned the small group of Catholic intellectuals who had been seduced by the ideas of the Revolution. Then in June 1848 Mgr Affre was killed at the barricades. Montalembert rejoined the camp of the orthodox who were to prepare the election of Louis Napoleon, and the latter re-established the rights of Pope Pius IX, whom Mazzini's Republicans had expelled from Rome. Shortly after that, Pius IX drew up *Quanta cura*, then the *Syllabus*, condemning all modern errors, democracy, liberalism, Socialism and Communism. The dogma of papal infallibility was promulgated at the First Vatican Council.

Then came the Commune, which executed its hostage Archbishop Darboy of Paris. The Church was wholly on the side of the Royalists and of moral order. The return to a philosophy of eternal essences was affirmed by Leo XIII in *Aeterni Patris*, making Thomism the official philosophy of the Church. *Rerum Novarum* completed the process in condemning Socialism, and striving to affirm the principle of a distributive justice derived from Aquinas, in a society of immutable hierarchies.

But how, at the beginning of the twentieth century, was it possible to hold strictly to Thomism? Neo-Kantianism, Bergsonian vitalism and materialism, menaced Christian society. In his encyclical *Pascendi*, Pius X condemned "modernism" as a whole. Henceforth, Rome saw Thomism as the sole anchor of salvation. Pius XII dedicated himself anew to the task, by drafting *Humani generis*, which condemned evolutionary theories as a "most pernicious" modern error.

8. This position became insupportable in the long run, in face of the progress made in the physical and human sciences (especially in linguistics and history). Although science introduced the destructive idea of relativity into the theory of knowledge, with positivism it also substituted for the affirmation of the infinite freedom of man that of the implacable determinism of universal laws.

Positivism had triumphed with the initial rise of capitalist civilization but, at the end of the nineteenth century, the sense of the historical relativity of capitalism (which Marx ascertained), and the discovery of the relativity of physical laws (which Michelsen's experiment led to in 1887), initiated a profound crisis in Western thought, which became the source of a partial renewal of Christian faith; its basis was to be totally different from the religious thought of the nineteenth century.

This crisis took the form of a reaction against rationalism. Boutroux had begun it in 1876 by writing *On the contingency of the Laws of Nature*. William James and Bergson completed it.

The way was open for Christian thought to develop a revolutionary self-consciousness as a Church whose function was no longer that of a divine magisterium, embodying a divine "essence", but that of an assembly of believers communicating only in the faith of Christ. Religion becomes, in the extreme case, "alienation from faith", to use Ricoeur's expression. Bergsonian intuition led quite naturally to that. Bergsonianism was included by Pius X in his condemnation of modernism. Two profoundly opposed intellectual currents thus emerged, expressed, say, in the faith of Péguy and the religious thinking of Merry del Val, Pius X's Spanish secretary of state.

Faith came to be identified with a "lived" psychological experience. The existentialisms of Berdyaev and Gabriel Marcel enriched it even more, while Edouard Le Roy declared himself to be a Catholic philosopher and heir of Bergson.

In reality, Pius X was right: the new self-image of faith resulting from the existential position, and which dated from the *Données immédiates*, by its fundamental irrationality (leading to the refusal to grasp the real world through the intelligence) stood for a deliberate ignorance of historical time. "The present" again became "eternity", which is all that "exists" in this psychological time in which past and future are projected into the immediate. Man is amputated from his past and future history, and since the Church is located in historical time, Christian history becomes "alienation from the faith". At the same time Marxism opened up an immense perspective for human history: that of the progressive and total abrogation of human alienation throughout history, and by history.

Catholic thought had to try to restore to the Church all its weight in the history of the world, an identification between the plane of natural and human history (as the biological and human sciences progressively outlined them) and the plane of sacred history (dominated by the suprahistorical myth of an external finality towards which the universe was tending). Teilhard tried it: but the opposition at the outset between the idea of a finality previously affirmed and scientific history *a priori* repudiating any finality, rendered impossible the determination of a common standard between the plane of science and that of the faith. Teilhard the scientist could become Teilhard the believer only by ceasing to be a scientist. The discovery by structural linguistics of the deep structures of the mind were to show the twentieth century how in reality these two attitudes, necessarily irreducible one to the other, revealed the persistence in the unconscious of a synchronic and mythizing structure which, until Marxism, was the dominant structure of the human mind) and of an integrally diachronic structure dependent on a realization of the unique reality of historical time, which appears in our time, in the eyes of the historian, the biologist and the astrophysicist, to be the only conceivable dimension of nature.

Surely this contradiction which the Church experiences on the doctrinal level reflects the gigantic class struggle of the twentieth century, and expresses the contradiction between a scientifically analysed history (whose movement has been apparent for a century in the growing activity of the working class and of oppressed nations) and an external finality to which the Church is linked, since God alone is thought to be able to place himself outside history and the class struggle?

This tragic perception of the Church's destiny has inclined the most lucid theologians to centre the Christian problem on the personality of the Christ-man by cancelling the Father-image. But the figure of the Christ-man, in its mythical aspect (which must be distinguished from the question of its historical actuality), in fact also contradicts the scientific conception of history founded on human mass behaviour.

More than ever, it seems impossible to escape the dilemma of choosing between a mythically structured and a diachronically structured conception of the world.

Translated by Verdant Green

Joseph Hajjar

Church History and Consciousness in the Eastern Churches of the Arabic World

SEVERAL different expressions are used to emphasize the local character of the Churches of the East: "national Churches", "Christian communities", "Eastern Churches", or "Eastern Patriarchates". These terms are perhaps also ways of stressing, by antithesis, the fact that all these Churches are very much part of the Catholic Church. The Eastern Churches see themselves as originating from a particular tradition among the ancient patriarchal sees.[1]

It is certainly true that the diversity of traditions and jurisdictions, going back over a thousand years, has served to crystallize their sense of the particular. There are many social and religious factors to explain this situation, but a number of historians persist in regarding it as a cause of heterodoxy or separation, and so the originality, vitality and permanent—sometimes universal —values of the Eastern Churches have tended to be disregarded or rejected in major works of Church history.[2]

Arabic (or Arabic-speaking, as a Western view would have them) historians have recently reacted to this exclusive tendency by showing greater openness to the major ecumenical tendencies now apparent in all the Christian Churches. Their research and reflection, in accordance with the life and mental approach proper to a community, have tended to concentrate on certain

[1] Y. Congar, "Quatre siècles de désunion et d'affrontement. Comment grecs et latins se sont appréciés réciproquement au point de vue ecclésiologique", in *Istina*, 1968, pp. 131–52.
[2] G. Alberigo, "New Frontiers in Church History", in *Concilium*, Sept. 1970, pp. 68–84 (American edn., vol. 57).

lines: these need to be rapidly sketched in this first systematic appraisal of historical activity in the last fifty years, or since the fall of the Ottoman Empire (1917–1920).

The pundits of Eastern religion have of course produced an impressive body of work, but their aims and approach, not to mention their ideology and methods of working, have generally been alien to the human and religious situation they are analysing.[3] There is no space here to provide an exhaustive list of Eastern historians, although there is as yet no critical bibliography of them, and the production of one would be of great interest. I can only give the main concerns of each, indicate their general approach, and place them in their particular Church tradition.[4]

Historians, one has to remark at the outset, are mainly interested in their own Churches, their own "confessional nations", their own Patriarchates. And so, with a few exceptions, the body of their work provides histories of the Church of Antioch, of the Maronite Church, of the Syrian Church of Antioch, of the Melkite Patriarchs, of the Church of St Mark, and so on. These works are not translations or adaptations of ancient chronicles, but original works, evidence of a real renewal of historical activity, a newly-felt need to go back to the sources, to read them with today's eyes and in the light of today's scholarly

---

[3] This view, which seems both negative and radical at first sight, is to be discouraged. See A. Laroui, *L'idéologie arabe contemporaine* (Paris, 1967), which severely criticizes the historical aspect of Orientalism, particularly the section dealing with "The Arabs and continuity", pp. 73 ff.

[4] It should be remarked that Christian Arabs write either in their native language, or in a foreign one, according to the needs of their cause or the requirements of their publishers. Some interesting recent titles are: Assad Rustum, *The Church of the City of God. Antioch the Great* (in Arabic; Beirut, 1952–58, 3 vols.). P. Dib, *Histoire de l'église Maronite* (Beirut, [2]1962). P. Daou, *History of the Maronites* (in Arabic; Beirut, 1970). This derives from Mgr Dib's work, despite its scholarly pretensions and fairly disagreeable polemical tone. Sewerios Yacoub Toumah, subsequently Patriarch Ignatius Yacoub III, *History of the Syrian Church of Antioch* (in Arabic; Beirut, 1953, 1957, 2 vols.). The Patriarch later published various monographs based on Syrian sources in his *Patriarchal Review* (Damascus). Gerges al-Mardini, *The Dawn of Christianity* (in Arabic; Beirut, [2]1963). A. S. Atiya, *A History of Eastern Christianity* (London, 1969). J. Hajjar, *Les chrétiens uniates du Proche-Orient* (Paris, 1963). H. Zayyat, *The Melkite Greeks in Islam* (in Arabic; Harissa, 1953).

methodology. Aims and methods may still be somewhat limited, but a real attempt is being made to rediscover an ecclesial identity and to give a reasoned justification for the origin of particular Churches. This concern for truth and rehabilitation is undoubtedly a sign of confessionalist revival at a time when all cultures are in the melting-pot. It is an exaltation of pluralism springing from a common origin—from the See and tradition of Antioch in particular.

Historians find in this multiplicity a value that may have contributed to divisions, but that has for centuries also been a bulwark against anti-Christian and often repressive political and socio-cultural domination. This has been the rule in a region that has always been a cross-roads of ideas and civilizations, a staging post of intercontinental exchanges at all levels. This rediscovery of Church consciousness seems to go with an effort at psychological tolerance and confessional liberalism. This may seem paradoxical to the observer little versed in the existential situation of the Near East, in view of the quest for authentication of traditions, but is none the less a fact.[5]

There is also the often sharp consciousness of belonging to the divided Church of Christ, but here the theological and juridical criteria used are not the same as those of the West. While theological reasoning is of course not ignored, the accent is on cultural diversity: the sacred attachment felt for the inalienable patrimony of the socio-cultural soil: religious regionalism, such as that of the deep strata of the Coptic population, of the astonishing age-long vitality of the Syriac substratum, of the rigid but catalytic impact of Armenian nationalism, of the mystical mountain cult, and of Libyan monasticism. All this predominates, even in the serious works of recognized experts. Another factor is the particularly strong Melkite feeling of attachment to the Byzantine tradition.

The old quarrel over Antiochan legitimacy is sometimes revived, and there is a fairly sustained campaign from outside the region to remind people of the largely forgotten patrimony of

[5] Alberigo, *art. cit.*, writes that the advent of a *global history* of the Churches, and local communities is urgent. This is what we are groping towards, slowly and hesitantly, but none the less with some encouraging signs.

the Syrian East. Stress is occasionally laid on the primatial rights of the See of Antioch, as a Petrine See and one of the notable centres of missionary activity of earliest times. These memories exalt a mentality steeped in the glories of the past, and this sort of nostalgia can often blind people to the ecclesial needs of the present. Repeated attempts to rekindle the long-deadened historical glow of the Syrian and Antiochan patrimony have met with no success. But experience has not led to the attempts being abandoned; historians are now exploring a new technique of rediscovery based on researches that have led to successes in the fields of monography and textual criticism.[6]

The ecclesiastical history of Palestine is almost completely ignored. Consciousness of a specific and authentic heritage seems to be inhibited for several reasons: the Orthodox patriarchal See and hierarchy, not to mention the clerical élite, constitute a monopoly of the Greek Confraternity of the Holy Sepulchre, which is foreign to the country and sets itself limited, though valid, objectives. The Latin patriarchate, for its part, is founded on ideals and theological and cultural expropriation. Finally, socio-religious attention seems to be fixed exclusively on the implantation and expansion of Zionism, with its political and military consequences. Arab Christians are no longer interested in the Holy Places, pilgrimages, the monasticism of the desert of Judea, or the theological and liturgical splendours of the Holy City, even as memories. And it was a Muslim with the highest professional qualifications who made Palestinian Christianity relive a whole epoch of conflict by the introduction of Protestantism in the nineteenth century.[7]

The Alexandrine patrimony seems to devote itself solely to bringing out the advantages of the Coptic tradition. It was, of

[6] The review L'Orient syrien, previously published in Paris, unfortunately ceased publication in 1956. The new Maronite university of the Holy Spirit in Kassalik seems to want to follow in its footsteps. Its review Melto became Parole de l'Orient in 1970. Antiochena, a roneoed review circulating in Rome during the Council, failed to live. This sort of desire to give Antioch its original importance once more is not new: see my remarks on the Eastern bishops at the First Vatican Council, in "L'épiscopat catholique oriental au premier concile du Vatican", in Rev. Hist. Ecc., LXV (1970), pp. 423–55 and 737–88.

[7] A. L. Tibawi, British Interests in Palestine, 1800–1891. A Study of Religious and Educational Enterprise (London, 1961).

course, high time for the admirable renewal of the Church in Egypt to spread into the field of historical research. Now the apostolic nature of the See of St Mark, and the originality of a Christianity so deeply rooted in the social and cultural soil of the region, are the features stressed.

These divided Churches also feel themselves in a very special way to be Churches of the martyrs, and so permanent signs of witness. It is almost as though the historians had all conspired to emphasize this common constituent of their historical experience, so alive in the sense of this reality in the minds of the learned and simple alike. For example, in symposia edited by a committee under Protestant patronage, the evocation of martyrdom and of the principal martyrs is a constant leit-motif, and the one common denominator linking authors who had not consulted each other beforehand and who come from very different Church backgrounds.[8]

This sort of collaboration across Church frontiers on the scholarly level is a particularly significant novelty. It shows that while the era of mutual distrust and systematic, insidious polemics is not absolutely over, there is a movement towards the opening of a dialogue, and tentative steps towards working together. The scholarship and character of research workers and writers, and the fact that a new academic generation is not confining its Christian commitment to confessional boundaries, particularly in the field of ecumenical studies, promise a time of mutual enrichment in the field of this aspect of historical consciousness.[9]

Interest in the remote past still seems to take precedence over concern for modern and contemporary history.[10] Could this be

[8] Committee of Christian Writers, *The Dawn of Christianity* (Beirut, 1956), and particularly, *Christianity in the Light of Day* (Beirut, 1957, both in Arabic. See also, *Al-Massara*, the Melkite Arabic review which published a series of ecumenically oriented historical articles. Between 1952 and 1959, a *Bulletin d'orientation oecuménique* was published in Beirut in French and had a considerable influence.

[9] The American University of Beirut has sponsored a joint work, *Arab Thought over the Past Hundred Years*, which studies all aspects of its intellectual development. The contribution on Christian Arab thought is by Mgr Ignatius Hazim, "The preoccupations of Christian Arab thought since 1866". The whole work, in Arabic, is a rich collection of valuable essays.

[10] B. Homsy, *Les capitulations et la protection des chrétiens en Proche-*

an attempt to escape from facing up to the problems posed by historical development, which have produced the present situation? Of course modern history has benefited from the valuable and sometimes definitive inquiries made in the field of chronological reconstruction,[11] and the publication of documents previously held in private hands or in secret diplomatic collections has had a beneficial influence on many intellectuals and churchmen of the Catholic East by giving them, in the light of the past, a better understanding of their true character and dignity.[12]

This rediscovery of the sources, however, is still in its infancy, and historians still find their task beset by any number of difficulties. Their work represents an often overlooked aspect of the struggle between a consciousness built up on historical myths entertained by official historiographers, often writing in the West, and a consciousness emerging from a true understanding of the history of the Church.[13]

In conclusion, would it be paradoxical to speak of the future? Knowledge of the past determines the modalities of the present, inspires their initial elaboration, and prepares the way for the future. The true historian is a craftsman of the future: committed to the truth his own vision of the past shows him, he works in a perpetually evolving world whose dynamism rests on a deep organic continuity. I hope that in our task, whose breadth and aims give us a role as valuable as it is demanding, we can come to see this existential richness, and to understand the responsibility attaching to the job in hand, whose basis is making the works of the past live again.

Orient aux XVI, XVII, XVIIIe siècles (Harissa, Libya, 1956). P. Raphael, *La rôle du collège maronite romain dans l'orientalisme aux XVII et XVIIIe siècles* (Beirut, 1932).

[11] See particularly J. Nasrallah, *Catalogue des manuscrits du Liban* (first three vols., Harissa, 1958–63); *idem, Chronologie des Patriarches melkites d'Antioche de 1500 à 1634* (Jerusalem, 1957).

[12] A. Rabbath, *Documents inédites pour servir à l'histoire de l'Orient chrétien* (Paris, 1910–12).

[13] If I may be allowed to refer to certain works of my own, see J. Hajjar, *Un lutteur infatigable, le patriarche Maximos III Mazloum* (Harissa, 1957). *idem, L'Europe et les destinées du Proche-Orient, 1815–1848, Unité arabe—Mission chrétienne—La question syro-libanaise et syro-palestinienne* (Paris, 1970).

Translated by Paul Burns

Ioannis Anastasiou

Greek Church History

THIS paper is concerned with the ideas of the historians of the period of Turkish domination up to the beginning of the present century.

After the Fall of Constantinople, the Eastern Orthodox Church —apart from the Russian Church—was in a state of subjugation. Because of illiteracy, it was very difficult for historiography to develop; during the seventeenth century, the scholars were concerned with dogmatic themes. Some chronicles were composed, but their fixed purpose and content deprived them of a general view of Church history.

By the end of the seventeenth century the need for a Church history was felt and in the next century two remarkable works were published, one in 1715 by Dositheos, Patriarch of Jerusalem, and the other in 1783 by Meletios, Metropolitan of Athens. Their authors took information from Byzantine historians, but they also profited from Church histories written in other languages.

Historians in the nineteenth century had the benefit of the progress of history in Western Europe and wrote scholarly works which used some scientific method and showed a knowledge of theories of history; Chrysostomos Papadopoulos wrote a work of this kind in 1909.

Meletios and Dositheos considered the study of Church history useful, for it impressed divine law in its readers' souls and thus protected them from their enemies; it was very important for the training of character and exercised a moral influence.[1] Papadopoulos' opinion on the use of history came very close to that of his predecessors. He saw it as depicting facts as they had occurred, and therefore as affording objective, real knowledge.[2] A Church historian was a faithful servant of truth and an impartial judge, but must also be a faithful Christian; for anyone alien to Christianity could not depict the Church's past correctly,[3] since its history manifests sacred things belonging to God.[4]

There were also differences with regard to the nature of the Church. Meletios wrote that the Church had existed since the time of Adam, but was made clearly manifest and perfect at the time of Christ's coming: hence Christianity was an historical fact and a central point of world history. There were two cities in this world, the city of God and that of man; they were connected and the study of one was inconceivable without a parallel examination of the other.[5] A modern writer like Papadopoulos recognizes clearly that the Church is an independent, self-sufficient organization with its own inner life. The conduct and actions, word and mind of the Christian are different to those of men of this world.[6] Christ founded the Church on earth; it is concerned to inspire mankind with true piety and the correct and philanthropic way of life.[7] The Church is the subject of divine mercy in the world. Men belonging to the Church are members of the body of Christ. The Church divines rightly the word of truth, and is one, holy, catholic and apostolic, as is apparent from its teaching, divine institutions, the sanctification of the Holy Spirit and the tradition which it preserves unadulterated. In this way, the Church reveals the heavenly Jerusalem and is the ark of salvation.[8]

One author at the end of the nineteenth century, Kyriakos, said that the Church had contributed to the sanctification of its

---

[1] Meletios, Metropolitan of Athens, *Ecclesiastical History* (Vienna, 1783), vol. I,XIII,XVI, p. 42. Dositheos, Patriarch of Jerusalem, *History of the Patriarchs of Jerusalem* (Bucharest, 1715), p. 9. Chrysostomos Papadopoulos, *Introduction to Ecclesiastical History* (Jerusalem, 1909), p. 29.

[2] Chrysostomos Papadopoulos, *Fundamental Laws for Ecclesiastical Historical Research* (Alexandria, 1914), p. 7.

[3] *Ibid.*, pp. 19, 22.   [4] Meletios, *op. cit.*, p. 2.
[5] *Ibid.*, p. 3.   [6] *Ibid.*, p. 2.
[7] *Ibid.*, p. 2.   [8] *Ibid.*, p. 45.

members and made it manifest by the moral regeneration accomplished in the faithful. Christians' faith had to show that they were unstained by sin, and in their works they must practise Christ's teaching about loving one's neighbour.[9] With the passing of time, the first purity and saintliness were diminished, although in the Christian community there were men and women who testified to the beneficent influence of the Christian faith and showed charity in their actions.[10]

In all this Church history, the inner sanctity of the Church reveals itself as the measure of historical judgment. The following opinions taken from Meletios, Dositheos and Kyriakos will make this clear. Cruel persecutions were inflicted on the Church by its pagan enemies, but it managed to survive and, being liberated, enjoyed every liberty and prerogative given by the Christian kings.[11] But, with the passing of time, the Church in Byzantium was enslaved to the State, although certain clerics, defending its liberty, resisted the kings.[12] In the West the clergy became tyrannical and wanted to dominate political and religious life in general, for the nations of the West were barbarous and at that time it was only the Church which preserved education, and experience and knowledge of lawful order.[13]

In addition to those external enemies of the Church, there were enemies within, half-Christian heretics who came from darkest pits.[14] They are described as insane, blasphemous, abominable, bringing to the Church impiety, tumult, disorder and schisms. Donatists were turbulent, agitators, liars and obstinate.[15] Schisms are created by the rupture of the bond of peace, are fed by envy and quarrels, and are worse than idolatry.[16] The Church and the Fathers, being of the opinion that heretics were led astray by the devil on account of their vainglory and arrogance, formulated orthodox doctrine on the basis of Holy Scripture and sacred tradition in the ecumenical councils convened by the emperors. Therefore heretics and schismatics are now streams disconnected from the fountainhead.[17] Papadopoulos, however,

[9] A. Diomedis Kyriakos, *Ecclesiastical History* (Athens, 1897), vol. I, p. 99.
[10] *Ibid.*, vol. II, p. 156.
[11] Meletios, *op. cit.*, p. 425.
[12] A. D. Kyriakos, *op. cit.*, p. 422.
[13] *Ibid.*, vol. II, p. 210.
[14] Meletios, *op. cit.*, p. 203.
[15] *Ibid.*, p. 326.
[16] Dositheos, *op. cit.*, p. 966.
[17] *Ibid.*, p. 966.

says more positively that heretics gave the opportunity for a clearer development of doctrine[18] and ought to return to the Church by repentance, not force. The Church has no relation with idolatry or with other religions, which are false. Mohammed, for instance, created a monstrous chaos, having mixed Christian and Jewish elements in his teaching; his religion is joyful in a perverted way and pleasant to those who are addicted to pleasures.[19] But the Church has an obligation to members of other religions who have been led astray; for this reason it endeavours by missions to bring them within the flock of Christ.

Although the Church was one and apostolic, the Great Schism came forth from the innovations of the Bishops of Rome, as well as their arrogance and despotic pretensions.[20] Other causes also contributed to this, such as differences of opinion and the way of life between Eastern and Western peoples, and scholastic theology, which tried to reconcile dogmatic truth with the reason of thinking man.[21] Since then, the two Churches have followed different paths, and our writers' histories have an anti-Roman polemical character. This is dominant throughout the work of Dositheos, Patriarch of Jerusalem. It is stressed that the Church is apostolic, not Petrine or Roman, that it has its apostolic constitutions and the sanctification of the Holy Spirit, in contrast to the Roman, which acknowledges as monarch and head the Bishop of Rome and has introduced heresies and innovations, having strayed from the one, catholic and apostolic Church. In this Church the clergy became dominant, and the worldly power of the Pope was introduced to counteract the power of princes to whom the Popes did not wish to be subjected, because they wished to rule the entire Church and the State. The clergy became tyrannical and sovereign,[22] and stopped the laity doing what lay within their competence.[23]

The reunion of the two Churches became difficult because the Roman Church wished to dominate the Eastern Church, and the emperors wanted to use it to help their political and military

[18] Meletios, *op. cit.*, p. 428.   [19] *Ibid.*, vol. II, p. 156.
[20] *Ibid.*, p. 319. Kyriakos, *op. cit.*, vol. II, p. 31.
[21] Kyriakos, *ibid.*, p. 260.   [22] *Ibid.*, vol. I, p. 426.
[23] Meletios, *op. cit.*, vol. II, p. 445.

schemes.[24] In this way, the so-called "Unions" brought disturbances and scandal, because peace which is far from truth causes enmity and alienates from God.[25] If union could be achieved in a genuinely godly way, then the Pope would be the first Patriarch.[26] But the developments in the Western Church in the nineteenth century brought it into collision with a multitude of scholars (whose scientific tendencies were regarded as dangerous) and with governments (whose rights and liberties were questioned).[27]

Differences with the Protestant Churches had been apparent since the sixteenth century and Protestantism with its extremes and many divisions[28] was considered a collection of heresies, and an impious labyrinth, but its appearance was thought to be most important.[29]

The Eastern Orthodox Church has stood in the middle, preserving incorrupt the ancient teaching and apostolic tradition, being a pillar and strengthening of the truth.[30] Such, at least, has been the polemical view of our historians, owing to the work of Roman Catholic propaganda among the Orthodox.

Another characteristic historiographical theme is that of the close union between the Orthodox Church and the Greek nation. This consciousness is clearly developed and reaches its peak in the works of nineteenth-century writers. More recent authors like Papadopoulos do not differ very much from their older colleagues. From their works we may extract the following opinions: Already in older times the Eastern Orthodox Church has been closely connected with Hellenism, which through Christianity had undergone a transformation and thus had made a new conquest of the world.[31] After the schism of the eleventh century, and particularly after the Turkish conquest, the Church was regarded as the saviour of the Greek nation. Through its clergymen, who were excellent apostles of Hellenism and Christianity,

[24] *Ibid.*, p. 127.　　　　　　　　　　[25] *Ibid.*, p. 163.
[26] Dositheos, *op. cit.*, p. 5.
[27] Kyriakos, *op. cit.*, vol. III, p. 7.
[28] Chrysostomos Papadopoulos, *On the Greek Ecclesiastical Chronography of the XVIth Century* (Alexandria, 1912), II.
[29] Dositheos, *op. cit.*, p. 1156. Meletios, *op. cit.*, vol. III, p. 426. Kyriakos, *op. cit.*, vol. III, p. 253.
[30] Kyriakos, *ibid.*, p. 17. Papadopoulos, *Introduction*, etc., p. 28.
[31] Papadopoulos, *Fundamental Laws*, etc., p. 6.

the Church preserved the Greek people in their faith and national consciousness.[32] If union of the two Churches had been achieved there would have been a danger of the Greeks being Latinized, as was the case with the inhabitants of Calabria and Sicily. Therefore Bessarion and those who agreed with him were considered traitors to Hellenism and the Orthodox faith.[33]

With regard to moral judgment in Church history, there is not much difference between older and more recent historians. Moral aberrations are to be observed in the West as well as in the East. Those of the West were emphatically stressed by our historians and ascribed to the corruption of the clergy and monks, and their neglect in teaching Christians ethics. The prevailing fanaticism, intolerance and persecutions of Jews and Moors were condemned, as well as the Inquisition from the fires of which new heresies had sprung.[34] Yet John Huss and Savonarola were praised as virtuous men. It was stressed that in the West the genuine, philanthropic and tolerant spirit of Christianity was misunderstood. There were also moral weaknesses in the East— especially in Byzantine times. During the Turkish domination, persecutions and repressions brought people close to the Church,[35] but there were also moral aberrations owing to a lack of instruction and learning among clergy and laity. However, the Church exercised a great and benevolent influence on the whole of the community. After liberation from the Turkish yoke, it was expected that the restoration of the Church would be achieved by an improvement in theological learning and the scientific development of its historical past, without any interruption of the genuine and true Orthodox tradition.[36]

[32] *Ibid.*, p. 26. Kyriakos, *op. cit.*, pp. 19, 17.
[33] Kyriakos, *op. cit.*, vol. II, p. 121.
[34] *Ibid.*, p. 285. Meletios, *op. cit.*, vol. III, pp. 82, 319, 180.
[35] Kyriakos, *op. cit.*, vol. II, p. 56; vol. III, p. 78.
[36] Papadopoulos, *Fundamental Laws*, etc., p. 27.